Justice for Marlys

Justice for Marlys

A FAMILY'S TWENTY-YEAR SEARCH FOR A KILLER

John S. Munday

University of Minnesota Press

Minneapolis — London

Published by the University of Minnesota Press
111 Third Avenue South, Suite 290
Minneapolis, MN 55401-2520
http://www.upress.umn.edu

Library of Congress Cataloging-in-Publication Data

Munday, John S.
    Justice for Marlys : a family's twenty-year search for a killer /
John S. Munday.
        p.   cm.
    ISBN 0-8166-4457-8 (hc/j : alk. paper)
    1. Wohlenhaus, Marlys Ann, 1961–1979. 2. Ture, Joseph Donald.
3. Murder — Minnesota — Afton — Case studies. 4. Serial
murderers — United States — Case studies. I. Title.
    HV6534.A335M86 2004
    364.152'3'0977659 — dc22

                                                        2004016226

Printed in the United States of America on acid-free paper

The University of Minnesota is an equal-opportunity educator and
employer.

12 11 10 09 08 07 06 05 04   10 9 8 7 6 5 4 3 2 1

For Marlys

Contents

Preface

*O*N THE AFTERNOON OF MAY 8, 1979, Fran Loux arrived at her home in Afton, Minnesota, a quiet rural community near the Wisconsin border, and found her eighteen-year-old daughter, Marlys Ann Wohlenhaus, lying bloodied and unconscious in the family office, the victim of a brutal attack. Just minutes earlier, Joe Ture, a serial rapist and killer, struck Marlys repeatedly in the head with a blunt object and left her to die. Fran, an emergency medical technician, could do nothing to save Marlys. Two days later, without a miracle and despite every medical effort, Marlys died and her wish to be an organ donor was honored. For more than seventeen years, Marlys's murder was left unsolved.

Fran and I had merged our Saint Bernard kennels about two years before Marlys's murder. At the time, I lived twenty miles north of Afton in Forest Lake, Minnesota, with my three children, JD, Maria, and Shawn; Fran lived with her daughters, Marlys and Lynn; her son, Ray Wohlenhaus, lived in nearby Houlton, Wisconsin. A year after the murder, Fran and I were married, and we moved with our children into a house where we tried to find meaning in the face of the most difficult loss to endure: the death of a child. We lived in fear of the unknown. Seeking to distance ourselves from that fear and the place where this horrible crime took place, we soon moved to Pennsylvania, and we eventually found ways to understand mourning and find healing.

In time we realized that we needed to find justice for Marlys. When our children grew up and left home, Fran and I began a renewed effort to solve this murder. Marlys died at the hands of a serial killer who slipped past the law during a three-year crime spree. When conventional police procedures failed to find the killer, we put pressure on law enforcement, increased public awareness of the crime, persuaded investigators with new approaches to join the case, and became a presence that would not be denied. In refusing to allow this crime to remain unsolved, we stand strong as part of a new phenomenon in America: victims who have been ignored and are fighting back.

I wrote this book to tell the story of how we kept our family together despite overwhelming grief, our frustration with the bungled murder investigation, and our knowledge that Marlys's killer was still out there. This book is for victims, to encourage others to demand justice for their loved ones wrongfully taken from them. Everyone who knew Marlys, or would have known her had she lived, has suffered an unimaginable loss. Our story shows how our family eventually succeeded in bringing about justice in order to heal after that violent crime.

This book is also for survivors. Fran and I, and all of our family, have good lives, although they are radically different from what we would have had if an evil, senseless act had not changed all of us forever. Fran and I continue to do "bereavement work" by writing, facilitating grief-sharing sessions, and visiting those who mourn. Solving Marlys's murder brought Joe Ture to justice for five other murders he committed, and several women who were assaulted by Ture were able to face their attacker in court. Many of his victims are heard in this book; in some cases their stories are told for the first time. Having done the last thing on earth we could for Marlys—ensuring that her killer will never have the opportunity to take another life—we hope we have honored her and the other victims.

This book is nonfiction. None of the events, acts, or words spoken here is made up or imagined, and none of the names has been changed. In 1979 I began to keep records, fill notebooks, clip articles, and collect photographs that form the underlying foundation for this book. I acquired more than four thousand pages of court transcripts from the many hearings and the trial of Joe Ture. I interviewed most of the main characters in this story, listened to interviews of others, and personally attended the court sessions. Law enforcement agencies provided time lines and transcripts of interviews. I made notes to preserve what I heard and saw. In compiling this account of our family's experience with murder, I endeavor to give a voice to others who have experienced the murder of a loved one and to give hope to those who still seek justice.

Part I

Murder

1

A Place in the Country

IN MAY 1979, Marlys Ann Wohlenhaus lived in Afton, Minnesota, with her mother, Fran, and her sixteen-year-old sister, Lynn. Marlys radiated graceful energy; she was lively and animated like a floating butterfly. Pretty like her mother yet more petite, maybe an inch or so over five feet tall, she weighed about one hundred pounds. Marlys wore her shoulder-length sandy blond hair parted in the middle. She almost always had a smile on her face and would often say, "If you see someone without a smile, give them yours."

Marlys enjoyed casual time with her friends. She made plans for a trip with her mom and her sister after her high school graduation, just three weeks away. Marlys dated guys who showed her respect and went out with groups of guys and gals. After she turned eighteen, she sometimes met her friends across the St. Croix River at a dance club called Dibbo's in Hudson, Wisconsin.

Three evenings a week, Marlys worked as a waitress at the Gene Daniels Restaurant in St. Croix Beach, just outside Afton, diagonally across the road from Greg's Body Shop, her step-father's business. The restaurant, which could hold at most seventy patrons, was also near the Beach Bar, a local watering hole where some of the body shop and lumberyard employees drank after work. Marlys was originally hired as a dishwasher. Now she waited on customers in her uniform of jeans, a blouse, and a brown apron. Marlys enjoyed the part-time job.

Near closing time at Gene Daniels on Friday, May 4, Marlys waited on the few remaining customers. A regular shared jokes with her. In the back, the cook fried a hamburger. One of the owners sat in a corner booth with some accounting work. A man in his midtwenties came in and sat alone. Of average height and build, with 1970s sideburns, he wore jeans and a black leather motorcycle jacket. When Marlys came up to him, he said, "Hi. I seen you before."

"I don't remember you," she said, putting a place mat in front of him. "What'll you have?"

"How 'bout a date?" he said, his smile almost a sneer.

"No way," Marlys responded. "Are you going to order?"

"Yeah. Coffee. Hey, I could give you a ride on my bike when you're done tonight."

"Coffee's all you want?" Marlys said, ignoring his proposition, not sure how to take him. She did remember him, from Dibbo's. She didn't know his name but recognized him as a guy who stayed on the sidelines, not part of the crowd. At times she caught him staring at her.

Although Marlys didn't know it, others from the valley also recognized Joe Ture. Just a few weeks earlier, on a normal evening at the Beach Bar, Ture went up to Vince Cartony and said, "I need work. You got a job?" Vince, owner of a logging business, patronized the bar after work with his employees.

"Not now," Cartony said. "I'm not hiring."

Ture asked Cartony several times more and finally Cartony became irritated. "Get lost. I told you, I don't need anybody."

"Well," Ture replied, "you should." Then he left the bar.

Half an hour later, Cartony walked to his new work truck at the south end of the parking lot. Ture stood by the truck as Cartony approached. Shocked, Cartony saw that all the marker lights around the perimeter of the truck bed had been broken. The last one, up by the driver's door, had a shorty Pabst beer bottle sticking out of it. "What the hell is this?" Cartony shouted.

"I told you. Should have hired me," Ture said.

Cartony said, "I run a business and I don't want to deal with you now." Ture just grinned when Cartony got in his truck. For a long time, Cartony would remember the eyes, the look of hate in Ture's face. He didn't trust him.

Neither did Marlys. At the Gene Daniels Restaurant, Ture continued to stare at Marlys. She said something to the cook, who looked over but didn't recognize him. Marlys took her time, filled the cup of a local resident, cleared the place where another customer had just left, put the tip in her pocket. Finally she took the coffee to her new patron.

"Here," she said and turned to leave.

"I got some real good dope," he said as he reached for her arm.

"No way, creep," she said, stepping back. Hands on her hip, she said, louder than she needed to, "You're a sicko."

Joe Ture turned red in the face. "It's a fair trade," he said. "Dope for a roll in the hay." He played with the coffee cup, spilled some coffee on the place mat.

"You are really sick," she said and went back to the cook, Eddie Thomas, who came over to the table quickly while Marlys told the owner what the man had said. Thomas told Ture to leave.

Ture claimed he didn't do anything but try to talk to her.

Thomas said they would call the cops if Ture wasn't out of the café in one minute. The owner had gone to stand by the telephone, and the man who knew Marlys also stood up.

Joe Ture left, wagging his index finger at Marlys when she called him a scumbag. Outside, he revved his motorcycle over and over before he finally drove off. Later, when Marlys finished work, she thought she saw the motorcycle behind her. She took a roundabout way home and figured she lost him.

Named Helen Frances Pruden at birth, Fran migrated to Minnesota in the late 1950s. She had married Jim Wohlenhaus, a Yankee who brought her to the Midwest from her hometown of Richmond, Virginia. The young couple began a family and lived in various apartments in Minneapolis. Their firstborn, Ray, came along in 1959. Marlys and Lynn were born in 1961 and 1963. In 1965 Fran and Jim rented a house in Afton, but five weeks after the move Jim told her he was leaving her. He said he couldn't raise the children in the style he thought they deserved. He left her with three little children and the advice to call a car repair expert named Greg Loux if she had car problems.

When her car broke down, Fran did call Greg. A relationship developed and led to marriage and the purchase of land on Trading Post Trail. This gravel road with hills and valleys served as Afton's border with the farmland to the west. Fran and Greg built the house in 1968. Fran loved the field at the top of the property, especially at sunrise when it glowed radiant and beautiful, with wild daisies and milkweed. For the family and for the deer, pheasants, and rabbits that visited regularly, the field was paradise.

Fran managed myriad activities while helping run the family business, Greg's Body Shop. She often delivered a finished car, picked one up for repair, or drove to get parts, as well as handling the book work. She learned public speaking when she became charter president of the Lake St. Croix Mrs. Jaycees. In 1978 Fran completed training to be a licensed emergency medical technician; she was the first Minnesota woman who was not also a firefighter to be an EMT.

During that decade, Fran began to raise and show pedigreed Saint Bernards. Greg's initial interest in the dogs faded, and Fran went to shows with her mother-in-law. Grandma Gert, as the children called her, treated Fran as a daughter and on several occasions helped mediate the increasing tension between Fran and Greg.

Though her marriage to Greg had bad moments even before the house was completed, Fran struggled to make the relationship work. In time they tried pastoral and professional marriage counseling, but their life together deteriorated. Sometimes Fran found herself in the woods near the house, alone but for a devoted Saint Bernard.

In April 1979, Greg had moved out, temporarily, to an apartment he rented. Fran began to fill the back room with household possessions she sorted and separated, as part of her pending divorce from Greg. He would get the house, the acreage she loved. Soon she would move out, with Marlys and Lynn. She knew she would miss the land more than the buildings, the bounty of nature, but not the years of strife. She had to give up her place in the country.

By May 1979 I had a relationship with Fran that we hoped would lead to something permanent. Fran and I had gone to a dog show in Madison, Wisconsin, over the weekend, so Fran had no idea that Marlys had been hassled at her job. After the show on Saturday morning, the two of us met my parents in Beloit, Wisconsin, on the Illinois border. They had driven up from their home in a Chicago suburb. Fran wanted to meet Mom and Dad, and I wanted to show Fran the place where I lived and worked before I moved to Minnesota.

I met Fran in 1970 when I went to my first dog show, also in Madison, to exhibit a Saint Bernard puppy. My wife, Joan, and I lived in Beloit and were novices in the competitive world of dogs. Fran had come down from Minnesota with her mother-in-law, Gert. Joan and I must have looked like rookies, against a wall, back from the action. Fran walked over to us, prompted to give us some helpful advice along with a smile. This is a nice memory, even though it may be enhanced over the years in our retelling of our first moment. I clearly recall thinking I didn't like culottes, even on an attractive woman like Fran.

A year later, Joan and I moved from Wisconsin to Forest Lake, Minnesota, north of the Minneapolis–St. Paul metropolitan area. I had made a change that enhanced my career, from a rural one-company town to work in a major city. I said we would like Minnesota if all the people were as nice as the woman we had met in Madison. Joan and I remained involved in Saint Bernard–related activities. We raised puppies, lost and sometimes won at dog shows, scooped kennels, and attended dog club functions.

The second time I saw Fran, at a Christmas party of a purebred dog organization in Stillwater, Minnesota, there must have been fifty people at the party. We didn't speak until she and Greg were practically out the door and on their way home. Someone introduced us, said we had Saint Bernards in common, and she said, "So you're Jack Munday." I had an opportunity to put a name to her face, and I regretted not having more time to talk with her. She wore a long white skirt with a white satin blouse. Her sparkling blue eyes shone with a radiance I will never forget. After that our paths crossed in mutual interests.

That Saturday in May 1979, after the dog show and our visit with my parents, Fran and I drove back to her house on Trading Post Trail. We talked about the weekend and relaxed in the living room before I went back to my home. By this time Joan and I had divorced and I had won custody of my three children.

Lynn was spending the weekend with her girlfriends, but Marlys came home around 10:00 p.m. "Come on in, Marcie," Fran called, using her pet nickname for her daughter. As Marlys sat in the living room with us, Fran saw a chance to talk to Marlys with me present. Fran told her about our time with my parents. "Jack and I have possibilities," she said. Marlys, not at all surprised by her mom's words, quickly looked for an engagement ring.

"It's still too soon for that," I said.

Fran said, "When the divorce is over, if I ever marry again, it will be someone like Jack."

Marlys interrupted. "What do you mean, 'if'? You will marry Jack." Then she looked me right in the eye and said, almost scoldingly, "All I want is for Mom to be happy."

"That's what I want for her, too," I said.

"Good," she added, showing pleasure at the beaming smile on her mom's face, then looked back at me. Marlys and I had grown closer as my relationship with Fran had become more public. "I hope I don't have to call you Dad." Her biological father, Jim, the man she and her sister called "our father who art in Houston" had abandoned his family. She didn't hate him or even hold his desertion against him. Greg, her soon-to-be-ex-stepfather, made her call him Dad.

I mumbled something stupid about how she could call me anything except late for dinner, a trite joke I immediately regretted. I should have welcomed her, hugged her as a daughter, even kissed her lightly to seal the pledge.

After a while, Marlys went to bed, happy for her mom but not sure what to say about the hassle at work the day before. She had also seen the "creep" this evening, at Dibbo's when she met her friends. But her mom didn't need more problems. Marlys also saw her brother, Ray, at the club and told him she needed to talk about something. He would know what to do. Maybe the guy would leave her alone, now that he had been tossed out of the café.

Late in the afternoon on Sunday, May 6, 1979, Marlys picked up her friend Jackie Beedle. Marlys and Jackie had been friends since early grade school and often did things together. That evening, the two girls drove aimlessly for a while. Marlys suggested a trip to Mahtomedi, a nearby town where a boyfriend lived, then changed her mind. The romance wasn't intense. "I don't want to go there tonight," she said. Jackie just shrugged. She understood that something was bothering her friend. "Let's stop at where I work," Marlys said. "Becky is supposed to start there soon. Let's see if she's on tonight."

At the restaurant, the girls went to a back booth, away from the entrance and close to the kitchen. When Jackie tried to talk to her, Marlys snapped at her, then got quiet and wouldn't talk. Marlys repeatedly glanced at someone in one of the other booths. She seemed upset, so Jackie turned to look. A man she didn't know, in a black leather jacket and baseball cap, seemed to be watching them, staring at her friend. His sunglasses sat on the table. Marlys got more nervous, and then about ten minutes later got up to leave without saying why. "I just want to go," she said.

"Do you know that guy?" Jackie asked.

"No, no. It's nobody," she said.

Jackie followed Marlys out, deliberately walking directly past the guy. He looked away. When she joined Marlys in her car, Jackie said, "Why don't you just take me home? I don't feel well."

Right away the girls saw someone on a motorcycle behind them. He stayed behind them and soon was right on the tail of the car. Jackie clearly saw the driver—the same person she had seen in the café. His baseball cap stuck out from his helmet. When they pulled up near her house, Jackie said, "Just keep going." She didn't want him to know where she lived. When they circled around the block, the biker followed for a while, then disappeared. The girls stopped briefly, and when they no longer saw him, Marlys took Jackie home.

"Call me," Jackie said to Marlys. Inside, Jackie told her mom, "A stranger followed us on a motorcycle." She later confided to her dad, "He's creepy and made Marlys nervous."

Marlys came home after dropping Jackie off. Fran and I had spent the day as partners occupied with little chores. We repaired a rabbit cage, tended to the Saint Bernards. Marlys said hello but then—out of character—went into the living room and sat quietly on the couch, turned so she could look out the window. From there she could see part of the driveway as it twisted past the dog runs I had moved from my house, then past the pole barn and finally out of sight where it joined with another family's driveway, then junctioned with Trading Post Trail. She may have been watching for a headlight.

Before I left, I came up the stairs from the lower level to say good-bye to Marlys. Her expression puzzled me. "Something happen?" I asked.

"Nothing," she said, turning back to the window. "I just feel like being quiet."

Later, after I had gone home, Fran came up from doing a load of laundry and went to the window. "How are you today?" Fran asked. "Are you feeling okay?"

"Sure, Mom. I'm fine," Marlys said. Marlys said nothing more that night, just sat on the couch until she went to bed. Oddly, Fran remembers, her daughter wasn't smiling.

2

A Butterfly Is Crushed

TWO DAYS LATER, May 8 began as a normal day for Marlys. She said good-bye to Fran and petted Patience when she let the Saint Bernard back in the house. Marlys drove her 1978 white Datsun B-210 coupe—a red bandanna tied to the rearview mirror—down the driveway, waved to the other Saint Bernards in the kennels. She drove past the pole barn, the playhouse, and the plot where the old dogs were buried, on by the neighbor's house and the school bus shelter, out the driveway onto Trading Post Trail, three-tenths of a mile.

The few weeks left until graduation couldn't pass fast enough. Marlys felt a happy excitement about life after high school; travel and relaxed fun were her main agenda. She went to her classes, laughed with Becky, Beth, and Denise, three of her best friends. After school, Marlys gave Becky and Beth a ride home. On the way she stopped at Greg's Body Shop to pick up the mail for Fran. Marlys spoke with her brother, Ray, and said again she needed to talk to him about something important. "It'll have to wait," he said. "I have to leave for the airport to pick up Greg."

"See ya later," Marlys said as she drove off with Beth and Becky. When they got to Beth's house, Marlys asked if the girls wanted to come home with her. Neither did. Marlys said she would come back to join them after she had taken the mail home.

Before Marlys arrived home, Joe Ture had come up the driveway from Trading Post Trail. He drove his dirty, cluttered Mustang directly to the house. Satisfied to see no car, he parked, waited a bit, then went inside the unlocked house. Patience ran up the stairs to Fran's bedroom when he came in. A shy and gentle dog, she almost always avoided people she didn't know. Ture followed her, found her in a bedroom, and pulled the door shut. Then he went back to the lower level and waited. Soon he heard the sound of a car. He looked out the window, recognized Marlys's Datsun, and hid in a ground-floor room.

When Marlys pulled up to the house, she parked in her normal spot. Used to seeing cars from the body shop and car business, she ignored the cream-colored Mustang parked in her mom's place. Marlys came in through the unlocked side door on the ground level. Upstairs were her bedroom and the refrigerator and the bathroom she normally used, all places one would expect an eighteen-year-old to go when she got home from school. Because she had the mail from the body shop business, however, Marlys walked past the stairs and into the tiny office with its huge rolltop desk, filing cabinets, and partially packed boxes.

Marlys placed the mail in the usual spot on the desk. Then she turned, perhaps heard a sound. Ture came at her, struck her with a metal object, hit her head, crushed her skull, splattered brains and blood, bone and tissue, broke several of Marlys's fingers when she raised her hands in useless defense. She slumped down, fell against a child's school desk as Ture continued to pound on her though she lay against the desk, helpless. He struck her head seven times. Then he left. He didn't take the money lying on the desk, didn't steal the CB radio on the ledge by the door, though it did tempt him. Upstairs, Patience heard the commotion, barked excitedly, dug frantically at the bedroom door.

Ture drove away slowly to avoid attracting attention. When he got to the fork in the road, he saw a little girl walking her bicycle up the hill. He spun gravel, raced out the driveway, and drove north. Miles from Afton, he threw the weapon off a bridge in South St. Paul. Later he went to work at the Ford plant.

Nine-year-old Angela Oswald, a fourth-grader at Afton-Lakeland Elementary School, got off the school bus at her home on Trading Post Trail about 3:00, then called her mom and changed into play clothes. By 3:15, she had gone out to play with her best friend. Angela rode her bike south on Trading Post Trail, which, just after her house, becomes a long, drawn-out hill. In the middle of the hill, Angela got off and started pushing her bike. She never could make it all the way up to where her friend lived.

When Angela reached Fran's property, she noticed a car coming out of the driveway. She wasn't really paying much attention, but when the car got to the end of the driveway the driver hit the gas and fishtailed, throwing rocks and dust, frightening her. The car sped down Trading Post Trail and out of sight. Because she had been so startled, she noted only that the car was light colored, and sporty, not a family type like her parents owned. Once the dust settled, Angela continued to her friend's house, promising herself she would tell her dad at supper that night.

Moments later, Fran arrived at the spot where Angela saw the car. Fran stopped at the entrance to her driveway and looked at her watch. Lynn's school bus wasn't due until 3:40. Ten minutes was too long to wait, so Fran continued up to the house. She saw Marlys's car and smiled in anticipation of seeing her daughter.

When Fran went inside, Patience didn't greet her, which gave Fran a moment of pause. "Marcie," she called out. "Marcie, I'm home." No answer. Fran walked past the CB radio on the ledge, put her packages down on the stairs, and walked into her office. Marlys sat motionless on the floor. "Oh, my God!" Fran screamed. "Marlys! What have you done?"

Marlys lay in a pool of her own blood, slumped against a school desk from Fran's childhood that was used as a table in the office. Blood was spattered everywhere. After finding Marlys's faint pulse, Fran grabbed the telephone from the laundry room and calmly called the sheriff's office for help, giving her name and instructions, asking for police and an ambulance. When the dispatcher asked her to repeat the information, Fran shouted, "Just send the ambulance! Don't waste time!" Frantic now, Fran bent to her daughter, held her. Then she grabbed the phone off the desk and called me, saying words that will forever echo in my head: "Jack! Oh, Jack! It's Marlys. Come now. If I ever needed you, I need you now."

Fran slammed the phone down, held Marlys close to her, soothed her as she waited for help. Outwardly calm again, Fran tried to think of something, anything, that would save her daughter. "Mom's here. It will be all right." The gentle words of assurance were all she had to give.

Deputy Don Schoenberger was the first to respond to Fran's frantic call. At 3:37, he pounded on the front door. Fran yelled, "It's locked. Come around the side. Go to the side door." Finally he did. When Schoenberger came into the small office, he eased Fran aside to check Marlys for signs of life, then tried to stop the massive bleeding.

Moments later Kris Peterson and another EMT arrived, going in the side door Peterson knew would be open. When he heard the call, he recognized the address. He had dated Marlys, and Fran was his regular partner on the rescue unit. Now he was coming to her house on an emergency call.

Peterson saw Fran, felt relief that she was okay, then, as he entered the small office, saw Marlys. He heaved a chair up onto the big desk, tossed some boxes back against the far wall. *Gunshot wound* had flashed into his mind because of the way the call came in, but as he gently reached for Marlys's head, he instantly saw that physical trauma had caused the head wounds. Putting aside his feeling of anguish, he immediately realized this was a "load and go" situation. "Bring the gurney!" he shouted. "We've got to get her to the trauma center. Get an IV set up," he shouted back as he tried to stop the bleeding. "She's lost too much blood. And get the shock trousers."

More rescue workers continued to arrive, and they brought the gurney as far as the hallway. It wouldn't fit in the small room. Peterson and Schoenberger put Marlys's limp body on a backboard, then onto the gurney. They took her out to the ambulance as quickly as they could. While they moved Marlys out the door to the ambulance, Fran stood numbly, watching them. "Oh, Kris! Please take care of Marlys," she said. Another rescue worker took Fran upstairs.

Lynn had heard the sirens and seen emergency vehicles passing as her bus came down Trading Post Trail. When she walked up the driveway, more cars flew past, other EMTs and police coming to the scene. Her first thought was that some-thing had happened to her mom.

Fran paced back and forth at the living room window, watching them load the gurney, then saw Lynn walking up the driveway. "Oh, my God!" she screamed. Whatever must Lynn be thinking, Fran worried, with the ambulance, fire trucks, squad cars, and unmarked cop cars scattered everywhere? Her stepson Kevin Loux, a volunteer firefighter who had come when he heard the call, stood nearby, having been told by a deputy sheriff to go upstairs with Fran. "Kevin, get Lynn," Fran said, desperate to have her daughter with her.

When Lynn came close to the house she saw the EMTs bringing someone out on a stretcher, mostly covered up. She couldn't see who they were carrying. She walked up to a deputy. "Who's being taken out?" she demanded.

Instead of answering her, the deputy, Tim Adams, started asking her questions. "Are you the younger sister? Has your sister been sick or had any falls?"

Lynn realized he didn't know what had happened and she walked over to Kevin, who hurried her inside. Lynn saw a crowd of people, not all in uniforms. She heard someone say it was Marlys who had been hurt and her injury was severe. She shook her head violently, thinking it couldn't be true, then heard one man say "homicide." One of the cops heard her gasp and said, "Wait upstairs."

When Lynn reached the top of the stairs, she saw her mother with blood all over her. "Mom, are you hurt, too?" she asked, panicked at the thought of both of them injured.

"No. It's from Marlys. I held her," Fran said. "I need to go to the hospital. Help me clean up."

"Is Marlys hurt really bad?" Lynn asked.

Fran said, "Yes, very bad."

Lynn asked, "How did it happen?"

"Somebody was in the house. We don't know who."

Lynn took her mother into Fran's bedroom, helped Fran out of her bloody clothes, washed her off, helped her get into clean clothes as quickly as she could. When they came out, Kevin said he would take Fran to the hospital. Lynn said she didn't want to go.

In the ambulance, the EMTs noted that Marlys still showed signs of life, though she had lost a lot of blood and part of her brain was exposed. She was still breathing, was a little combative, tried to move around. She fought them weakly with her arms once they had her in the ambulance. Marlys moaned when they did a second survey after they locked the gurney in place. They gave her oxygen, tried to hyperventilate her to keep the swelling of the brain down. One EMT bandaged the gaping hole on the side of her head while the ambulance raced off to St. Paul Ramsey Hospital. They made radio contact with the emergency room so the doctors would be ready.

After I got the terrifying call from Fran, I drove recklessly fast from my office in Minneapolis, through St. Paul and east to Fran's house, changing lanes, cursing at slower drivers in my path. I saw and heard an ambulance racing back to St. Paul. "It's Marlys," I thought, wondering what had happened to her that would make Fran sound so frantic. I could only speculate and go faster. After what seemed forever, I turned south on Stagecoach Trail, slid around the corner onto Valley Creek, skidded to a halt as I saw Fran in a car with her stepson Kevin. I pulled into his lane, motioning for him to stop. "I'll take you," I told her.

Fran got out and groped her way to my car as though she would faint. I held her arm, settled her in, and shut the door. I sped off to chase the ambulance, Fran huddled against the door. "What happened?" I asked. "I still don't know."

"Someone bashed her brains out," Fran said. "She was just lying there, against my little school desk. He hit her, over and over. I picked up pieces of her skull. I held her. Oh, Jack! I loosened her jeans, and she sighed. I think she recognized me. Jack, Patience was locked up in my bedroom. Whoever did this to Marlys put the dog in there. She must have heard it all. She was trying to claw the door down when I arrived." Fran began to sob. "There's no hope," Fran said. She sat coiled in the corner of the seat.

I kept looking at her, forcing myself to glance at the traffic, trying to stay on the road. "There's hope," I said. "They can perform medical miracles."

"But you didn't see her," Fran said. When we arrived at the hospital, I held her arm as we walked into the emergency entrance. Fran was beginning to go into shock.

When the emergency room personnel began their fight to save Marlys's life, their primary concern was the amount of blood she had lost. Because the doctors couldn't obtain any blood pressure, they immediately moved Marlys to the trauma room in the operating room suite. A nurse put in IV lines for transfusing her. Then the neurosurgery service took over.

Dr. Richard Gregory performed the initial procedures. He noted three cuts on Marlys's scalp: one in the left front, one on the right, and one in the back on the left. The star-shaped cuts exposed three skull fractures. The worst one was in the left front where the bone had been pushed in. Under the bone, the membrane had been torn. Brain matter seeped out through that opening. That fracture extended down into the eyeball's bony socket.

With profuse bleeding from all three wounds, Dr. Gregory's first order of business as he made his assessment was to continue the efforts to stop the bleeding. First he and his assistants used a small forceps to pinch off bleeding blood vessels, then used electric current to cauterize them. When that didn't work, they tried a special packing material designed to promote clotting. Each unsuccessful procedure left them with fewer options, and now the bleeding had become uncontrollable.

By the time they had gotten many of her wounds packed off, Marlys developed a blood-clotting abnormality caused by severe brain injury. While Dr. Gregory performed the surgery, her blood simply stopped clotting. Marlys now began to bleed not only from the injuries but from the IV sites as well. At that point the doctor concluded it was a hopeless situation and they closed her scalp. Marlys started bleeding from her nose and mouth. Dr. Gregory called in an ear, nose, and throat specialist to pack off that area. Her only chance now was for her brain to remain functioning long enough for her body to permit her blood to clot.

They put Marlys on a ventilator. She continued to receive blood and blood products during the night to maintain her blood pressure.

3

A Long Way to Fall

AT FIRST, the constant contact with doctors and our prayers for Marlys took precedence over our personal needs. Fran fainted several times and received medical assistance in one of the rooms in the emergency complex. Fran's son, Ray, arrived, bringing Greg from the airport. Marlys remained in surgery. The family didn't get a full report on her condition for a long time. Calls were made to relatives, and arrangements were being made for travel to Minnesota. The group grew quiet, deep in suspense, hoping and praying for a medical miracle to save Marlys's life.

Finally Marlys came out of surgery, still in a deep coma. Fran waited on every word from the doctors. The medical specialists did their best but never offered much hope, at first giving Marlys a 10 percent chance of waking, but not really believing even those odds.

Marlys lay in the critical care unit, hooked to innumerable tubes and wires assisting her breathing, giving her medicines and fluids, monitoring her vital signs and almost negligible brain activity. Greg left for a while and Ray went outside, smoking cigarettes and raging at the world. Fran and I began a vigil. We watched the monitors, ached to see some sign of life. Though she clung to every hope, Fran felt everything falling away.

When Fran had gotten out of Kevin's car to ride to the hospital with me, she had told Kevin to take care of Lynn. Kevin took her to the house of Marlys's friend Beth, where many of her sister's friends had gathered. Lynn's friends on the bus had seen the rescue and police vehicles. They had been calling her house, but the police had told Lynn to stay off the phone. When she got to Beth's house, she called a few friends to tell them that there had been an accident; she would talk to them later. Then the group sat in the living room, asking the same questions over and over. Lynn didn't know any more than she had seen.

Lynn found momentary solace at Beth's house. "Let's all sit down," Beth said when the group gathered. "Sit in a circle." One by one the friends said a prayer, recalled a memory, expressed a hope for healing. Everyone spoke. It was their way of coping. They knew Marlys was in bad shape.

Our vigil at Marlys's bed brought no improvement in her condition. At Fran's request, I made a call from the hospital. "I need to talk to Lynn," I said to Beth, who answered the telephone.

"I don't want to talk," Lynn said when Beth relayed the message. "I'm too upset."

"He says you have to go to the hospital," Beth said.

"I don't want to," Lynn answered.

"He says you have to be there," Beth said. "Marlys has a 10 percent chance and your place is there." Beth's mom offered to drive. I knew Lynn didn't want to see her sister suffering, but I also knew she would later regret not coming if, as we feared, these would be the last days or hours of Marlys's life.

When Lynn reached the hospital, she walked down what seemed to her to be a dark hallway and saw Fran and Ray standing outside a room. She hugged her mom, not saying anything, just looking into Fran's eyes, Lynn's mind burning with questions she couldn't ask. Fran took Lynn in to see Marlys and they stood by the bed. Lynn started to cry, and Fran said, "Try not to get upset in the room."

"How do you not get upset?" she answered. "Is she going to. . ."

"Don't!" Fran said. "Marlys can hear us. I know she can. We need to be positive." For a while then, mother and daughter just sat together and cried.

After the visit, Lynn, Ray, and some friends went into a private waiting room. At that time they were more worried about whether Marlys was going to live or die than about who had attacked her.

It is a long, long way to fall from being a friend, a lover, hoping to become family, to the outside, closed out by a tragedy. In the confusion at the hospital and the days following, when grief was so intense, other issues and selfish agendas intruded, violated the dignity due Marlys. Marlys, in intensive care, should have been everyone's sole concern. But she wasn't. At one point, Fran decided to stay in a hotel near the hospital. Greg wanted to talk about Fran's relationship with me. Finally Fran said, "This isn't about me. My daughter is dying and I don't have time for this." Fran walked away, heading for the room where her daughter lay hooked to the life support system.

I couldn't leave Marlys by herself that first night. I quickly drove Fran and Lynn to a nearby hotel, bought some things Fran needed at a department store, then returned to the hospital. Fran, exhausted and under medication, spent the night at the hotel with Lynn and Lynn's friend Karen, who had come to be with Lynn.

Fran found it difficult to sleep, seeing Marlys every time she closed her eyes. She tried to pray, *God, I'll do anything if you don't let Marlys die. Save her. Oh, God, are you punishing me? If I promise never to see Jack again, will you bring Marlys back to life?* Lying in bed, pushing her tear-washed face into the pillow, Fran sobbed. *Did I cause this? Is there any way . . . ?* Terror grabbed Fran, deep down in her heart. *Is this God I'm praying to a God who takes a daughter from her mother because of her mother's sin?* A spark glowed, dimly but present. *The God I pray to would never take Marlys to punish me. My God is not a God who would harm any human to punish another, no matter what the other person's sin might be.* Fran tossed in the bed, wondering what Marlys could possibly have done to cause another human to be so depraved. *I'll find that murderer,* she resolved, finally able to sleep.

After dropping the package from the store at Fran's hotel room, I went back to intensive care. I sat facing Marlys, staring at the monitors that refused to wake up. Indifferent machines confirmed the little life Marlys still had, lazily dispensing data, white lines on green screens, thin as the thread of life Marlys clung to. All I knew was that I had to be there. I suspect I tried to bring Marlys into recovery by force of will. I know I wanted to stay inside the family circle.

This was not the first time I had kept a solitary vigil at a young woman's bedside. As I watched the machine breathe for Marlys, I thought of Julie, my first stepdaughter, and her own short life. Julie had been born in 1957, five years before I met her, when Joan was seventeen. Joan's father and mother raised Julie, spoiled her, loved her in their way but kept Joan from raising Julie. When Joan and I married in 1962, though I tried, we never had the opportunity to be parents to Joan's daughter.

We had our own children in time: first John, in 1963, then Maria in 1965 and Shawn in 1971. Joan's parents moved to Canada and Julie went with them. With no supervision or guidance from a grandfather who thought everything she did was wonderful, Julie spun out of control as she sought adventure in what we later learned was a drug-influenced "if it feels good, do it" rebellion against conventional society.

Julie ran away from her grandfather to come to us for a short while in 1972. I tried to understand her need for independence, letting her decorate the room we provided for her. She burned incense, used a black light to highlight fluorescent scrawls on the black-painted walls. When she didn't come home from school, Joan and I both tried talking with her and imposed simple discipline like denying phone privileges when she stayed out all night. Finally, after being grounded, she left us, escaping out her bedroom window rather than using the unlocked front door, going back to Canada and her grandfather, eventually to be on her own at fifteen. Julie lived a short, tragic life, dying in a hospital in Winnipeg just after her sixteenth birthday when her liver couldn't respond to treatment of complications from hepatitis she contracted from sharing needles with her friends. Our being at Julie's bedside had not helped her survive.

The night of Julie's funeral, I thought about the choices we had made and the terrible end to a life unfairly shortened and unfulfilled. I broke into tears, sobbing and feeling more pain than ever before in my life. Then I remember thinking, "I've just grieved for Julie. It's over." I didn't understand Joan's grief and expected her to get over it as I thought I had. I had never felt that Julie was mine.

During my vigil with Marlys, over and over I thought of Julie lying in an isolation ward in a Canadian hospital, her liver failing as the hepatitis raged in her body. And I admit I worried about Fran and my tenuous relationship with her. Would I be any better at understanding Fran's loss if Marlys died? Would I grieve and then try to go on with life? Would Fran withdraw?

While Fran slept at the hotel and Marlys lay in intensive care, breathing with a ventilator, my thoughts were my only companion. The day of the attack I had called Fran's house to talk to Marlys, before her mom came home, because we were planning a surprise Mother's Day party. Marlys and I had a good relationship that had become close. The previous November, Greg's oldest son was married in a church wedding, and Greg told Fran she had an obligation to act out her part for the public, no matter what went on at home. Marlys insisted that I go to the wedding, demanding that I escort Fran's mother, Mildred Duty, who flew in from out of town for the wedding. Marlys wanted me to be there, seemed to need to be sure I'd be present to support Fran.

At the reception, when the evening drew to an end, I danced the next to last dance with Fran and the last dance with Marlys. At seventeen, she had boyfriends and family there, yet I held her in my arms as the party ended. I can still see her smile and her bright blue eyes looking up at me. She had her mom's happiness first in her heart at that moment.

I saw the same smile a month later at Christmas. The end of 1978 wasn't an easy time for Fran. I came to her house often, to cheer her up and do what I could to help. On one visit, I found Marlys sitting in her favorite chair in the living room. "What do you want from Santa?" I asked.

Marlys radiated a smile, saying, "I just want me and Mom and Lynn and Ray to be together for a nice evening." The twinkle in her eye was beautiful. "You could come, too," she added and laughed. But this wasn't a happy time. Emotions were more like the Minnesota weather: raw, cold, and even frozen, not joyful.

At Easter Fran cooked a nice dinner for Marlys and Lynn and Ray. I was there, too. Marlys sat in the same chair in the living room, and I said, "Looks like Christmas came at Easter this year."

"I know," she said, with the same wonderful smile, the same twinkle in her eye.

The thought of Marlys being happy brought me back rudely to the stark room in the hospital. The clock moved slowly, as regular as the ventilator keeping Marlys alive.

The next day, Dr. Gregory paid two visits to Marlys. The first was a routine morning call on rounds, when he noted that her condition had declined. He wrote that her outlook was poor. Fran had returned, trying to remain hopeful. Others began arriving to stand the vigil. Jim Wohlenhaus, Marlys's biological father, flew in from Houston with his girlfriend. Fran's mother came from Virginia with Fran's sister, Evelyn Burkhalter. There were meetings and discussions for much of the morning. Each new visitor came to the room and spoke words of encouragement to Marlys, still deeply comatose.

The nurses called Dr. Gregory back in the early afternoon. He found Marlys to have changed for the worse, neurologically. She had lost her ability to breathe spontaneously off the ventilator and her blood pressure had risen tremendously, indicating a huge increase in cranial pressure. The blood was trying to go up to her brain in spite of the high resistance inside her head.

Dr. Gregory performed a brain death exam at 2:35 p.m. Since she was deeply comatose, he tested some of the nerves that come off the brain stem. She had no pupil reaction; her pupils were fixed and her eyes didn't move side to side or up and down. She had no cornea reflexes, so that his touch to the surface of her eye produced no blinking. She had no facial movement in reaction to painful stimulation. When he touched the back of her throat, she had no gagging reaction. She didn't cough when he put a suction catheter down into her chest. When he tickled the bottom of her trachea, she had no reaction. She had no arm movement even with inflicted pain, though she did have a spinal cord reflex: she pulled her feet up away from his probing. He took her off the ventilator, waiting until she turned blue and had an abnormal heart rhythm, yet she made no effort to breathe. At that point, Dr. Gregory concluded that she had no function in the brain stem, the part that controls basic functions like breathing. Marlys was brain dead; she had met the criteria.

Dr. Gregory took Fran to a conference room. She had been outside the intensive care unit with me, trying to overhear what the medical team was saying. After a moment when Dr. Gregory seemed to be looking for words, he gave in to what he knew. "There is no hope," he said. "None."

"Is she dead?" Fran asked.

"Not technically, though there is no brain activity. None that I can find, I'm afraid."

Fran sat motionless, trying but unable to accept the truth of what the doctor told her. Reality made no sense. "How long can we keep her on life support?"

"It will be your decision as to when she comes off support," Dr. Gregory replied, "but it should be sooner rather than later. Actually," he added, "Minnesota law as well as St. Paul Ramsey Hospital protocol requires a confirmatory second exam twenty-four hours later. If it's the same as now, and I'm sure it will be, we will want your permission to disconnect her from the life support, and that will be it."

"She wanted to be a donor," Fran said, trying to hold on to some part of Marlys. "She has it on her driver's license." Her eyes pleaded with the doctor.

"We'll arrange that. And we'll put her on a heart machine, to preserve her organs. We can't take the chance that her heart will give out if she is to be a donor. Until tomorrow."

Another neurosurgeon did the next day's test, confirming Dr. Gregory's findings of May 9. The hospital kept Marlys on the ventilator and on the heart machine so that her wishes to be a donor could be honored. On May 10, 1979, Marlys was transported to the University of Minnesota Hospitals, where her life officially ended.

4

The Investigation Begins

JUST BEFORE 4:00 P.M. ON THE DAY OF THE MURDER,
not long after the ambulance and the rescue workers left
the house, Robert Ellert received a call while he was driving his
unmarked squad car. The dispatcher told him to go to Fran's
house. In the Washington County sheriff's department since
1971, Ellert had been promoted to the position of investigator.
In addition to having primary responsibility for the northern
part of the county, not including Afton, he also handled crime
scene analysis in the entire county. When he arrived at the
house, he spoke with Deputy Don Schoenberger. Deputy Tim
Adams stood by.

"I was first on the scene, Bob," Schoenberger told Ellert,
"and I didn't know what to make of it at first. I saw the mother
holding the victim, and I checked for signs of life. I helped the
rescue crew load her up. We screwed up the crime scene pretty
bad because we had to try to save her."

"Where's the mother?" Ellert asked, looking around. He
knew the body shop but didn't know the family personally.

"She's gone to the hospital. She came home to find her
daughter. God, I can't imagine how she feels. I almost got sick
myself." Going inside the house, Ellert and Schoenberger were
careful not to disturb anything. "The chair up on the desk was
the biggest thing they moved. Kris Peterson went in first. He
knows the family."

"She was that bad?" Ellert asked.

"I was sure she was dead when I first touched her," Schoenberger replied. He stood at the door while Ellert walked into the small office.

"There's a hell of a lot of blood," Ellert said, mostly to himself. He noted small pieces of bone and other matter coagulated in the blood. "Can't tell if this is tissue or something else," he said, bending down. "Look at all the blood spatters on the furniture. It's all over the books, magazines, and papers. Hell, it's even under the desk." Ellert backed out of the room.

"We've got a lot of work to do, Don," Ellert said, then called Sergeant Richard Neville and Detective Jim Richter, also of the Washington County sheriff's department. The two officers went outside to wait. After briefing Neville when he arrived, the investigators decided that Schoenberger would show the room to Neville, who would then take the crime scene photographs inside the house.

Ellert walked around the house to look for anything unusual. Near the rabbit cage behind the parking area where Marlys's car sat, Ellert found partial footprints. Ellert and Neville noticed recently trampled grass behind the cage, suggesting a path. "Think someone walked through here?" Ellert asked.

"Let's see," Neville replied as they followed the trail for about sixty feet. Then the path faded, though they couldn't tell if the person had turned back or if the grass was simply different.

Detective Jim Richter arrived soon after. His assignment, as investigator covering the area of Washington County from Stillwater south to Afton, put him in charge of the investigation. After a brief discussion with his colleagues and a quick look at the crime scene, Richter went to the hospital in St. Paul. "I'll talk to them all," he said as he left.

At the emergency room, he talked to each person, getting statements and forming first impressions. Richter considered each person a potential suspect, a possible killer. A short, swarthy man, he enjoyed investigating, especially when he could interrogate suspects who could be leaned on. He worked hard at his job. Initially he knew only that a victim had been badly hurt at the residence. He wasn't sure what kind of assault it had been. He knew that the mother found the victim, that the rescue people had transported her to the hospital, and that the victim's mother had come to the hospital on her own.

"I know this is difficult," he told Fran, "but try to tell me what happened." Fran again told the story of coming home, calling for Marlys, finding her, calling for help, calling for me, calling the body shop, screaming at the first officer, riding to the hospital. She felt faint, told Richter she needed to lie down. A nurse gave her a sedative.

Richter took each of the others aside and spoke privately about their relationship to Marlys, where they were when they heard about the attack. When Richter spoke with me, he learned that I had been at my office when Fran called me, making a note to check that out thoroughly. Richter had a longer conversation with Greg Loux. He obtained names of others who might have had an intense relationship with Marlys. Richter spoke with one of the doctors working on Marlys, even before the family did, learning the nature of the assault, guessing at the potential murder weapon. None of us noticed the subtle shift of attention from Marlys, the victim, to the unknown murderer.

Richter had been gentle with Fran, penetrating in his questions to me. With Greg Loux, he used a variety of approaches, seeking Greg's confidence, challenging him, not quite confronting him. Richter had already formed a first impression of who had committed the murder, or at least who was responsible, and he would stay with that theory for a very long time.

Returning to the crime scene, Richter instructed Deputy Tim Adams to remain at the house during the night. Adams hadn't been trained to investigate but would protect against curiosity seekers and preserve what evidence there might be. A large man, bulky and not at all smooth or athletic in movement, Adams had been nicknamed Lurch. He tended to blend humor with an intimidating aura. He combed his dark brown hair back and flat against his skull, exposing a prominent forehead. His large, straight nose and mahogany mustache punctuated much of what he said until his grin broke wide open to announce the punch line.

Adams sat on a couch in the living room, near the stairs to the bloody crime scene below. When Patience, who had been put back in Fran's bedroom, pounded her paw against the closed door, Adams called his supervisor, jokingly saying that he and dogs don't get along. "What am I supposed to do with the dog?" he asked.

"Well," his sergeant replied, "let the dog out."

Adams went to the bedroom door, opened it, and stepped back, hand on his billy club. The Saint Bernard looked at him with equal consternation. Adams cleared his throat and said, "Dog. Get out" to Patience, who then came out of the room. Adams went to the back door and opened it. Seeing that she had followed him, he said again, "Dog. Get out." Patience ran outside. About twenty minutes later, he went to the door and yelled, "Dog. Get in," and Patience came back into the house, returning to her sanctuary in Fran's bedroom. Adams sighed and stayed in the living room by the television. Later he would tell people, "Me and the dog were friends then."

On Thursday, Fran signed papers authorizing the removal of Marlys's life support. After she gave parental permission for her daughter to be an organ donor, Fran left the hospital. She and Greg went to the house to get her clothes and a dress for Marlys. They met Detective Jim Richter there. Richter had them walk with him through the house to see if anything might have been taken. Richter probed them for information about the several suspects whose names he had. Greg had suggested that Jeff Sullivan and Tom Cartony were at least potential suspects. He also mentioned a young man, Dennis Sipe, who hung out in the woods near the house. Several times Greg reminded the detective that he, Greg, had been on a flight from Chicago at the time of the murder. He had met a man seated near him. They had exchanged business cards and Greg bought him a drink.

When Greg talked, Fran stood silently by, barely hearing the words. Fear gripped her as she stood in this house that now seemed so evil. Could it be Greg? she wondered. This was her first thought about who might have killed Marlys. No longer hoping to save Marlys, she too began to think of who might have taken her daughter from her. She listened to him tell the cop all about an alibi. Even if it was true, she knew it would have been easy for him to get someone to do it. There are people who would kill for money.

"Tell me about Sullivan," Richter said to Fran.

"Jeff was Marlys's old boyfriend," Fran said. "A year ago they argued and then broke up."

"Has she seen him lately?" he asked.

"No. I don't think so," Fran said.

"Cartony," Greg said. "Tom Cartony lives right up the hill, or did. They have a big family. The kid is into drugs."

"Was Marlys?" Richter asked.

"No," Fran said.

"She may have used pot," Greg said.

"No she didn't," Fran shot back.

"I'll talk to this Cartony," Richter said. "We know about him anyway. Actually, I'm talking to everyone even remotely associated with Marlys and with the two of you."

"Find the killer," Fran said.

After the walk-through, a staff writer for the St. Paul *Pioneer Press* found Fran and Greg still at the house, getting ready to go to the funeral home. Richter told them to talk to the press because it would help the case to appeal to those who might know something to come forward.

Shaking and barely holding herself together, Fran agreed to talk to the reporter: "I could only think of the movie *The*

Godfather when they pulled back the sheet and there was the horse. It was the most horrible thing I've ever seen in my life." Greg walked away. Asked to describe her daughter, Fran told the reporter, "Marlys is a little butterfly, filled with love and laughter. Her one goal in life was to make me happy. If I was happy, she was happy." In response to a question from the reporter, Fran talked about going into her house and whether or not she could go back to the room where Marlys was killed: "I don't know, I'm not coping too well. No matter if I close my eyes or leave them open, I still see her the way I found her. Whoever did it had to be a warped and demented person."

Fran finally went to the funeral home to arrange for the wake and the funeral. Later that evening, she and Greg came to a dinner at the hotel where Fran and the out-of-town family stayed. Marlys's father, Jim Wohlenhaus, had gathered family and friends for the meal. No one had much to say as they ate. When Fran arrived, Jim briefly asked if the arrangements were made. He offered no comments on Fran's brief summary. The sadness of the evening, knowing Marlys would never join anyone for supper again, became reality for those at the table. Lynn left early, to be with friends. Jim's girlfriend excused herself. Fran's mother and sister went to their rooms. I went home.

On Friday evening, a two-block-long line of people gathered outside the door of the Jones-Bradshaw-Hauge Funeral Chapel in Stillwater to attend the wake. An eight-by-ten-inch framed high school senior picture of Marlys adorned the closed blue casket. I talked to Fran briefly by telephone during the afternoon. "I don't care what anyone says," Fran said, "you can come to the wake." I numbly accepted her permission, only later wondering what she meant. Our lives were a mess.

Fran received a steady stream of mourners. Off to one side, Greg stood, paced, watched. He wore mirrored sunglasses that concealed his eyes and the identity of those he watched most closely. Fran sat patiently, listening to words that failed to penetrate the wall she had set up to protect herself. One by one, young and old spoke sympathetic words that fell short of comfort. At the end of the evening, Fran faded off to the hotel with her mother, her sister, Evelyn, and Lynn.

The morning of the funeral was cloudy. It rained. At Greg's insistence, for the sake of appearances, Fran rode with him in the lead car, followed by Marlys's father, Jim, his girlfriend, and his brother's family. Next were Ray and Lynn. I drove behind them, with Evelyn next to me. In the back sat Fran's mother, Jim's mother, and Greg's mother. At the church the three grandmothers sat with me, two rows behind Fran. My three children sat just behind me. During the service, both Fran's mother and Greg's mother leaned on my shoulder. The Reverend Richard Borgstrom gave a memorial tribute to Marlys, not attempting to explain evil but celebrating the joy she brought to those who knew her.

During the reception at the church after the funeral, Reverend Borgstrom came over to me, offering his handshake. "I have to say this, Jack," he said. "I've heard some things from Greg about your relationship with Fran." I just looked at him. "But I've watched you through the time at the hospital. And since then. I don't think those things are necessarily true. I think this is different from what I've been told. I'd like to think you'll take care of Fran."

"I intend to," I replied, not sure if it was worth discussing allegations Greg might make.

"Can I give you some advice?" Borgstrom asked. "It's about the grief Fran will be enduring."

"Sure. What is it?"

"Let Fran talk about what happened. She's going to want to talk about it over and over, and you're going to be tired of hearing about how she found Marlys, how she hurts."

"Okay. I can listen," I said.

"But let her talk," Borgstrom added. "Be interested. Don't look bored, even if you are, and don't stop listening."

"Fair enough," I said. It would be advice I would be reminded of many times, especially when I forgot to listen.

I had made plans with Fran for her, her mother, and her sister to come to my home for dinner on Sunday. After taking my children to be with their mother because it was Mother's Day weekend, I waited for a call that never came, wondering, working furiously on repairs in the yard, full of frustration.

Instead of comforting the woman I love, I shoveled rocks and dirt into a low spot in my driveway. *I'm on a chain gang,* I thought, *prisoner for a crime I didn't do.* Maybe I didn't see Marlys lying against the desk, blood everywhere, her skull split open, helpless. Fran did, not me. I couldn't picture Marlys other than smiling, grinning. My mind would not let me go to that horror, not yet. Fran had crossed over into a world beyond my imagination, beyond any comprehending thought. When I looked at Fran at the church, I honestly didn't realize how deeply shock had gripped her. I just couldn't comprehend the depth of her despair nor the empty void in her heart. Fran could not close her eyes, even to pray, without seeing Marlys as she had found her. Healing had no meaning.

All I could do was relive Fran's frantic call and our time together in the car on the way to the hospital. I thought again about how I had called the house hoping to talk to Marlys about our plans to have a surprise Mother's Day party for her mother. The possibilities of what I imagined happening haunted me. Did Marlys go into the office to answer my phone call? Did the ringing phone cause the murderer to act? Was she already lying there, waiting for rescue, or did I call before she got home? I'd never know.

Fran didn't call. I telephoned and finally talked to Fran's sister. She was going back to Virginia. Fran had gone into hiding. And so when Fran checked out of the hotel, when she sent her mother and sister back home instead of coming to my house, I didn't understand. I didn't hear from Fran for three days, each an eternity, long and empty.

After the funeral, Fran stayed at the church, now trusting God to take care of her daughter in heaven. Ray stayed near his mom for a while, already blaming himself; Marlys had wanted to tell him something. "I'll never know," he told his mom, then told his father, "It sure will be some Mother's Day tomorrow." Ray hugged his mom and left.

If there was comfort for Fran at Memorial Lutheran Church that day, it came in human form. Gwen Peterson, who, with her husband, Len, was an active member of the church and a friend of the family, spoke gently to Fran. "Come home with us," Gwen said. "You and Lynn can't go back to that house, and you can't stay in a hotel forever. Come to our house. With Yvonne married now, Len and I have plenty of room." Gwen Peterson took Fran by the arm, led her to sit, away from the others.

"I don't know what to do," Fran said, looking over at Greg.

Gwen followed her gaze, saw Greg standing tall, appearing angry, talking to a man she didn't know. "Who is Greg talking to?" Gwen asked.

"Richter? He's a detective from Washington County," Fran answered. "I didn't know he was here." As if on cue, Detective Richter motioned for Greg to stay where he was, then walked over to Fran.

"Fran, do you know where you're going to be staying?" Richter asked. He looked at Gwen, as though to say more only if he had Fran privately.

"Gwen wants me to go to her house. She and her husband handle our insurance. They're members here. Len ushers."

"Where is your husband?" Richter asked Gwen.

"He's in the other room, taking down tables. I can get him."

"Please. Would you mind?" Turning to Fran, Richter said, "Will you feel safe with them? How well do they know Greg?"

"They're our friends. What do you mean about Greg?" Fran asked.

"For your own safety, you need to be somewhere where we can keep you under surveillance," Richter said. "I don't think you and Greg should have much contact for a while."

"Do you suspect him?" Fran asked. "I really don't want to talk to him now."

With Gwen gone to get her husband, Richter quickly told Fran that Greg had a motive, even though he had an alibi, because of the money involved in the divorce settlement. "The investigation will go better if you and Greg stay apart."

"We have a separation agreement," she said.

"Do you trust them?" he asked, pointing to Len and Gwen as they came back.

"Yes."

"Then take them up on their offer. We'll have a car near the area at all times."

"Am I in danger? Are they? Will they be in jeopardy because of me?" Fran shuddered at the thought of bringing harm to decent people. Finally, with Richter's assurance and Gwen insisting, Fran took Lynn to the Petersons' house.

5

Killing Chickens Wasn't Enough

*T*HOUGH WE DIDN'T KNOW IT THEN, the man Fran feared and desperately sought for murdering Marlys lived only a few towns away and occasionally came through Afton. Joe Ture worked in St. Paul and its suburbs as an auto mechanic, drifting from one job to another. Nothing would have happened to Marlys if police had made the right decisions back in December 1978.

Ture also spent time north and west of the Twin Cities. Clearwater, Minnesota, is a small community outside St. Cloud, mostly farms and country homes. When Alice Huling divorced her husband, she moved from suburban St. Cloud with her four children to a small white two-story house on land owned by Stearns County Deputy Sheriff John Dwyer. Dwyer lived nearby with his wife and had known Alice before her divorce. He liked to spend time with Alice's children, taking Wayne and Billy fishing or hunting. Occasionally he would drive Alice's daughters, Susie and Patti, home from school if they stayed late for gymnastics practice.

Susie attended Kimbell High School and worked at the Cozy Cafe on Highway 15 in Kimbell. Her shift coincided with the last classes at Kimbell High, as part of a school policy for student work. Early in the week of December 11, 1978, Joe Ture saw Susie, took a fancy to her, and asked her for a date. She told him she couldn't date anyone her mother didn't know, adding that, besides, Ture was too old. She walked away, nervous, anxious to go home.

At 3:00 p.m., when Susie's shift ended, Ture followed the school bus to the Huling home. Later that evening, he followed Alice to Southway Bowl, where he approached her and asked if he could date her teenage daughter. She refused in clear and not very pleasant language.

On December 14, 1978, Billy and Patti came home from school around 3:30 p.m. Alice had picked Susie up at the café after work, and Susie had made dinner by the time Wayne came home on the late school bus after wrestling practice. The children watched television and did their homework while Alice took a bath. That evening, Susie called Jan Ask, the owner of the Cozy Cafe, to tell Jan that she was upset with the man who had pestered her that day. Jan knew who Susie meant; the man looked like her brother.

At about 9:00 p.m., Billy said goodnight to his mother and went up to the second-floor bedroom he shared with Wayne, talking with him for a while until Wayne, whose bed was closer to the door, shut off the light. Susie and Patti had separate bedrooms, and Billy could tell that Patti's light was on. Susie had turned her light off.

During the early morning hours of December 15, 1978, Joe Ture came to the Huling house, angry at having been rebuffed by Alice. He parked his car on the side of the road, then walked into the yard, seeing the tan Volkswagen van parked partly behind the house. Alice had a flock of chickens she raised for eggs and the occasional chicken dinner. With her words ringing in his head, fueling his anger, Ture went into the hen house and began killing the chickens, one by one. Smirking at the thought of Alice finding the dead birds in the morning, he walked back to his car and drove off.

As he drove, Ture thought to himself that Alice had not been punished enough. Turning around, he returned to the Huling home. He put on his dark ski mask and went to the door, taking a loaded shotgun and his club, an aluminum rod wrapped with a leather steering wheel cover. He tried the door, found it unlocked, and entered the house, intending to rape Susie. He walked into the kitchen, noticed the toy cars on the table that Wayne and Bill had not put away. He casually picked up one of the cars, then tore out the cord from the wall-mounted telephone. Searching, turning on a light in the kitchen, he walked quietly and came to Alice's bedroom.

"Who's there?" Alice said. "What do you want?" She reached for her robe and got out of bed.

"Shut up," Ture said, threatening her with his club.

"I know you," Alice said, pointing at him. "You're the pervert from the bowling alley. You leave Susie alone. Get out of my house or I'll call the sheriff."

Ture punched Alice several times, knocking her back when his fist slammed into her head near her left eye. He beat her body with the club, striking her under her right breast, in the stomach, and on the right hip. When she wouldn't stop struggling, Ture shot Alice in the leg.

Upstairs, thirteen-year-old Wayne and eleven-year-old Billy were awakened by the noise. "What was that?" Wayne asked his brother, though both of them knew the sound of a shotgun. Then the light came on in the stairwell and the boys could hear someone coming up the stairs, slowly, one thudlike step, then another. Bill pulled his sleeping bag over his head, still peeking out at the doorway. The footsteps were softer now, on the carpet in Patti's room. Bill Huling then saw a man standing in the doorway. He didn't recognize Joe Ture, never having seen him before, but even in silhouette noticed the blue-black ski mask and that the man didn't seem tall.

"Who are you?" Wayne asked. Ture fired his shotgun at Wayne, striking him in the skull and left eye, killing him instantly.

Ture left the room and went to sixteen-year-old Susie's bedroom. Bill heard her scream, then heard a shot that struck her on the left side and crown of the skull, the shotgun blast tearing through the hand she raised in futile self-defense. Ture proceeded to twelve-year-old Patti's bedroom, working the pump action of the shotgun. "What's going on?" Patti cried out.

"It's okay, go back to sleep," Ture said, then shot her, blowing off the top of her head. After shooting both girls, Ture returned to the boys' room and fired at Bill, who had pulled the covers completely over his head, holding them above himself with both arms. The blast from the shotgun missed the terrified boy, passing between his head and his left arm, rocking the bed. When Ture poked him with the barrel, Bill moved slightly and Ture fired a second shot, miraculously missing again. Frozen still now, Bill waited for more but Ture left the room, stomping down the stairs to the first floor.

Ture went into Alice's room. "I want you to know they're all dead," he said to her, then shot Alice two more times, finally killing her.

Bill's ears rang so he couldn't hear much of anything, though he did hear the shots downstairs. At 4:15 a.m., according to the clock in his room, Bill got out of bed, glanced at his blood-covered brother, walked out, looked in Susie's room but didn't see anything because it was dark, then saw Patti covered with her blanket, blood all over. The family dog, Dusty, crawled out from under her bed. Bill crept down the stairs. He looked in the kitchen, the living room, then saw his mother in her bed. Running to the phone, he found the torn-out cord. Bill went back upstairs, got dressed, and carried Dusty downstairs. He put on his jacket, let Dusty out, and ran on the path that led to Deputy John Dwyer's house. Seeing boot prints and fearing the killer had gone to this house, too, Bill ran up the road to the Dirksens' trailer house. Bill pounded on the door but no lights came on. Jean Dirksen pulled back the curtain and told her husband, "It's Billy."

Steve Dirksen came to the door, asking Billy, "What's wrong?"

"Someone shot my family," Bill Huling shouted out.

"What?" Jean said, not able to understand.

"A man came in the house, shot Mom, shot Wayne, and Susie and Patti too," Bill said, then started to cry.

"I'll get John," Steve said, calling the deputy and leaving the house. Steve picked up Dwyer, and the two went to the Hulings' home. Dwyer saw what had happened and put in a call to the sheriff's dispatcher at 5:04 a.m.

After sending Dirksen home and asking him to call the local Catholic priest to come give the last rites to the victims, Dwyer waited for Deputy James Kostreba, who noted the hard-packed snow and ice on the Hulings' driveway. He entered the house with Dwyer behind him. Kostreba found a spent shotgun shell on the floor in the kitchen and another on the third step of the stairway.

Kostreba started up the stairs. Dwyer said he was staying in the kitchen, adding that "they were like brothers and sisters to me. I don't want to see them like that." The rescue squad arrived just as Dwyer came out of the home.

Inside, Kostreba went up the stairs, heard Susie gasping, and called for the ambulance crew. When the medic reached her, he found that she was doing "brain stem" breathing. He could not find a pulse, and at that moment Susie died. Once he was certain she was no longer alive, he and his co-workers removed Susie, Alice, Wayne, and Patti from the house, taking all four in one ambulance to the St. Cloud Hospital. All four bodies would undergo autopsies.

The next morning, not more than a few hours after the murders, Stearns County Detective Lou Leland arrived with a chief deputy. A hasp and padlock had been put on the door. Leland took photographs of the outside of the home, then went in, taking photos of the kitchen and Alice's bedroom. He went upstairs, checking and photographing each crime scene.

In Billy's room, Leland determined that the shooter had fired slug projectiles at Billy, noting that they had passed through the bed and out of the house. Leland would later conclude that Bill Huling survived because, perhaps randomly, the shotgun shells fired at him had been rifled slugs normally used for deer hunting. The shells that killed Alice and Susie were number 4 buckshot. Patti died from a shell with number 6 bird shot. Shot like that scattered—it wouldn't have missed Bill like the slugs did. Leland used dowels and strings to determine the height of the killer, confirming the average height and making it unlikely that someone as tall as Deputy John Dwyer could have been the shooter. Dwyer, because of his relationship with Alice, had already become the primary suspect, even though Bill Huling would tell the police the next day that it couldn't have been Dwyer. "I would have recognized him," Bill would say. "I'm positive, because he would have filled the doorway. He's big, not like the guy I saw."

During his initial investigation, Detective Leland went back outside, checked the van and the chicken shed. He saw a few rat holes and two dead chickens. He also noted unusual foot-prints going to and coming from the house back to the road where he could see from snowmelt that a car had been parked.

On the morning of December 19, four days after the Huling murders, the Wright County sheriff's department dispatched Deputy Gary Miller to a restaurant at the Clearwater Truck Plaza in response to a complaint about a customer harassing a waitress. The manager met Miller outside and told him the person was inside, eating. He pointed to the 1971 Chevrolet four-door that the man had been sleeping in earlier. Miller read the tags and determined that the car had been listed as a stolen vehicle.

After the manager pointed out the customer Miller approached him, found out his name was Joe Ture, then asked him to step outside. When Ture said no, Miller said, "This isn't optional. We're going out."

"The car ain't stolen," Ture said. "I bought it from a car dealer in the Twin Cities where I worked until they fired me. I just ain't made the payments yet."

Miller took Ture to his car, handcuffing him when Ture tried to get something from the car. "Take it easy," Ture said.

After confirming that the car had been reported stolen, Miller arrested Ture for unauthorized use of a motor vehicle and placed Ture, still handcuffed, in the back of his squad car. Entering Ture's car to look for its keys and a newspaper Ture told him he wanted, Miller discovered a metal bar, wrapped in a steering wheel cover, on the front passenger seat. "Is this the newspaper you were planning to read?" Miller said, holding up the club. Miller didn't notice that the newspaper had the story of the Huling murders.

Miller seized the metal bar, took Ture to the Wright County sheriff's department, and arranged for Ture's car to be towed. Miller and another officer searched the vehicle, where they found a toy car and a ski mask. No shotgun or ammunition were found.

The metal bar and several of the items found during the search, including the toy car and the ski mask, were turned over to Deputy James Kostreba and Detective Ross Baker of the Stearns County sheriff's department, who were investigating the Huling murders. When Kostreba and Baker interviewed Ture on December 20, 1978, he said that he had been fired from his job a few days before and had been living out of his car.

Baker led the interview. "I noticed a little toy there. A little thing with Batman, was that also in the car when you got it, or do you recall where that might have come from?"

"It's mine," Ture said. "I got grandkids."

"Oh, you have grandkids?" Baker said, sarcastically.

"My daughter does. I'm uncle or whatever."

"Well, if your daughter has children, well, then you'd be a grandfather then, huh?"

"Yeah."

"How old are you?" Baker asked.

Correcting himself, Ture said, "No. I mean my sister."

"Oh your . . . ?"

"Uncle, yeah. Uncle."

"You are an uncle and then the children, they would be what, they would be your grandchildren or won't be his grand . . . ?"

"I'm the uncle. My sister's got kids, I'm the uncle, right?"

"Oh, I see," Baker said. "All right. And then you were around them after you picked up this car here?"

"Well, what is that, ah, difference that a couple of toys make?"

"Well, it might make a lot of difference. You never know. Huh. I just wanted to know if you know where that one came from, if it was in the car or not. Do you recall it?"

"No, I don't see where it makes any difference."

"Well, it could, though. It could make a difference."

"Well, until you prove it to me."

"Prove what? I mean, where you got it?"

"No. Till you prove to me what this whole charade is."

Baker concluded the interview at that point. Ture was charged with unauthorized use of a motor vehicle and released on January 4, 1979. No one showed Bill Huling the ski mask, or asked him about the Batmobile toy. Ture should not have been free to return to St. Paul, to stalk Marlys in Afton, to kill her.

The days that followed Marlys's funeral were almost more difficult than Fran could handle, and in some ways she shut down, stopped functioning. If she thought of Lynn or Ray, or even me, it was only out of a sense of obligation rather than because she wanted us at her side. How could she miss someone who was a phone call away when no telephone could reach Marlys? Guilt, too, stabbed her heart, not only from continuing tension with Greg about her relationship with me but also because she feared it might have given the perpetrator a possible motive.

Gwen Peterson continued to guide Fran, to give her little chores. She asked Fran to peel potatoes for dinner, fold laundry, write thank-you cards. Fran struggled to accomplish small tasks but found herself unable to concentrate. She sat for hours in the bedroom.

On the Tuesday after the funeral, Fran finally called me and asked me to take Lynn to the dentist. Fran couldn't concentrate on even that simple task. My talk with Fran at the Petersons' home might as well have been a conversation with a zombie. Fran didn't seem to hear what I said, so Lynn interpreted. In the car, Lynn answered my questions mechanically but offered nothing else. I didn't know what to say either.

Over the next week, Fran and I had more brief contact. I helped write a letter offering a reward, then moved our dogs to my house. On May 24, I stupidly took Fran to a dinner dance in Minneapolis for patent and trademark lawyers. As we rode along, Fran slipped off the wedding ring she still wore and held it out for me to see. "I really am through with him," she said.

"That thing should have been off long ago."

"Should have?" she asked. "Those words don't mean anything anymore. All I'm looking for is freedom."

At the party, we stayed by ourselves, sitting with people I worked with but not interacting with them. We barely heard the music, and we left early. We were both stumbling on the slippery dance floor of life, neither of us stable long enough to help the other. Fran's grief and pain for her murdered daughter overwhelmed any other feelings. I didn't know how to comfort her.

On the way home, Fran asked me to stop at the cemetery. Silent, we stood at the fresh grave. Fran fussed with the flowers. "I'm going to replace these with growing plants," she said. Then I took her to the Petersons' house, and I went home.

6

God, Why Are You Punishing Me?

DURING THE FIRST FEW WEEKS AFTER THE MURDER, the investigators continued to focus on local suspects. Detective Richter took Marlys's friends Becky and Denise in a squad car to a hill overlooking Fran's home. Richter scared them to try to get the girls to tell him about Marlys's boyfriends. He also asked them about Greg's relationship with Marlys and Fran.

When he was contacted by Richter, Greg signed a release for the telephone records of the body shop. Several of Greg's telephone calls to Fran were recorded by a deputy. Greg filed a claim for victim assistance, and for the proceeds of an insurance policy on Marlys's life. Lynn received title to Marlys's car.

Fran's friends Barb and Sandy Cobb invited her to their summer cottage at a lake in Wisconsin for the Memorial Day weekend. Lynn and her friend Karen went along. With their permission, Fran invited me to meet her at the Cobbs' cottage and to bring my three children. When I arrived, Sandy gave me a tour of the vacation home. The warm sunlight sparkled on the lake. Sandy took me for a brief sail on his sunfish sailboat. I found it hard to concentrate on the sailing lesson, wanting to be back on shore with Fran. The hot weather combined with overwhelming sadness kept everyone but the youngest children from much activity. Baking in the sun seemed the preferred response to the day. Even the blaring "Beach Boys weekend" music on a radio brought no enjoyment.

Ray rode his motorcycle up to see his mom. He came to the front door of the cottage, let Fran hug him, then stood there looking at her. "How are you doing?" Fran asked her son.

"How do you expect?" Ray said. "What are the cops doing? What are they doing to find the guy who did it?"

"They say they're working on it," Fran said. "I'm meeting them at the sheriff's office next week."

"A lot of good that will do." Getting back on his bike, Ray said, "Maybe I should talk to some of these guys myself. Maybe the cops aren't asking the right questions."

"Ray," Fran said, "let them do their work. They'll find the killer. We can't interfere. We might mess things up."

"That's easy for you to say," Ray replied. "I gotta do something. I'm the brother, remember? I wish to hell I knew what she wanted to tell me. I'm the one who saw her last, and she wanted to tell me something. Important."

"It could have been the Mother's Day party she and I were planning," I said. "She wanted you to be there."

"It was important," Ray said, "not something like that." Ray told Fran he was leaving, didn't want to stay, had some things to do. He left without coming inside.

Later, after dinner and a few more hours of aimless conversation, Fran and I walked outside to a bench by the water. Fran talked about Marlys and what she meant to her, how much she missed her. "No one can replace her," she said, crying softly.

"It will be all right," I said, knowing it wouldn't.

"Grandma Rose told me I have to let her go. Let her go to God or heaven. I didn't want to hear that," said Fran, now sobbing. "Jack, I wasn't ready to let her go. I had so many hopes for her. I wasn't ready."

The next day we came back to Minnesota in a two-car caravan, stopping for a root beer float along the way. Trying hard to be her old self, Fran said she knew a place to stop to get everyone a treat. But her eyes were so sad.

On the following Wednesday morning, Fran met Richter at the Washington County sheriff's office. He took Fran's statement, beginning with basic information: her age, where she lived and worked, her relationship to Marlys. Then he asked Fran to describe the events of May 8.

"I talked to Jack, and I told him that I would be coming into town. I walked out to my car, and Patience came out with me. That's automatic, and then when the weather is nice, I leave her outside while I'm gone. But this particular day, when I was putting my stuff in the car, she walked up onto the ledge, just before the rabbit hutch, onto the hill area, and looked around as if to say the sun wasn't even shining bright enough yet. It wasn't raining but it was still wet out. Then she turned around and came back in the house. So, I said, 'Well, you can just stay in all day.' I talk to my dogs. I'm not crazy, I just talk to my dogs. They understand me."

The interview lasted over an hour. Near the end, Richter shut off the recorder. "We still haven't cleared Greg. He's been acting strange, aggressive. I've heard the tapes of him on the phone with you."

"Do you think he did it?" Fran asked, now afraid again.

"No. Not him personally," Richter said. "He couldn't have. But we're checking out his alibi. And we're wondering, speculating that he may have had someone do it. It's just a suspicion right now." Richter held up his hand as if to stop her from actually accusing him. "This is only one lead of many." He closed the file. "Do you have a place to go? Somewhere out of state where you and Lynn can go?"

"I could go to Houston, to Lynn's father's place."

"Not there. If someone was looking for you they would check there. Is there another person you trust?"

Fran thought for a while, considered her family on the East

Coast, then remembered a friend she had helped when the friend's marriage had gone bad. Now she was happily remarried. This would be safe. "How about California?" she asked.

"Does Greg know the person?"

"He knows her from her first marriage. Her name is Jan, and she's got a nice husband now. But I don't think Greg even knows where Jan lives. She doesn't like him, anyway."

"How soon can you go?"

"Tomorrow," Fran said. "Lynn's out of school."

Fran and Richter called Jan, then Fran bought two tickets to San Diego under assumed names. Fran and Lynn would leave the next day; Barb Cobb would take them to the airport. Richter would have an unmarked car tail them, to see who might be following.

After leaving the sheriff's department, Fran met me for lunch at Ninos Restaurant, where we had our first date, nearly two years before. We needed to be at a place with good memories. Back in 1977, we had parked our cars in adjacent spaces at Ninos for a necessary conversation about the way our relationship had begun to change. I hurried over to her door. When she gathered her purse, I had leaned toward her to have that first kiss.

"Not yet," Fran said. "Let's go in."

I found a secluded table, seated her as if we were on a date, then took my place across from her. Our eyes locked, stayed true, and our smiles opened wide.

"How is your marriage?" Fran asked. "Are you happy?"

"No," I replied. "How is yours?"

"Not good," she said. "We've been to counseling, and it hasn't worked. I'm afraid of being a two-time loser." Marriage, not murder, occupied our thoughts back then.

We ordered, talked, and ate, filled each other in on when we married, what went wrong. That first lunch together ended with our being more than friends. We said we were soul mates. To say we were in love gave words to what had happened without our intending any kind of relationship.

This lunch in 1979, after Marlys's murder, had a much different tone. "The sheriff wants me out of state," Fran said, no smile to be found. "They have some leads and don't want to worry about my safety. I can't tell anyone where Lynn and I are going."

"No one?" I asked.

"They specifically mentioned you, along with Greg. And even Ray won't know." Fran gently put her hand on mine and said, "But here's the number where I'll be. Don't call. I'll call you. But I want you to know where I am. I do love you."

"I just want you safe. I wish I could do more."

"Give me time. That's what I need," she said. The next day she flew to California.

A week passed before I got a call from Fran. She had been told by the cops that she was not in danger: Greg had passed a second lie detector test. Fran and Lynn next went to Houston to visit with Lynn's father for a few days, and then flew to Padre Island, Texas, for some sun and relaxation.

On June 11, I went to Washington County to give a statement to Detective Richter. I also gave Richter the name and phone number of the co-worker who was in my office with me when Fran called me after finding Marlys. Later I called Fran to let her know how the interview had gone. We had several long phone calls.

On June 13, while we were talking, Fran said, "Padre is really neat. You'd love it here."

"I'd love it anywhere you are," I replied.

"Too bad you aren't here," Fran said, lifting my heart.

"I'll fly out," I said. "And I'll bring JD," I added, thinking that my oldest son and Lynn were only a year apart and would enjoy the beach together. JD had given Lynn his fishing knife for protection during her last few days of school before she left for California. I dreamed of merging the families, hoped stepbrothers and stepsisters could actually like each other. Marlys had been working on that already. With her gone, it didn't seem as possible.

The next day, I made airplane reservations to leave on the 15th, a Friday morning. After work on Thursday I drove to Afton, went to Marlys's grave, and watered the flowers as Fran had instructed me to do. In the background I heard sirens; I hoped that whomever the ambulance was taking to the hospital would have a better chance than Marlys had. When I got home, I called the hotel in Padre, began a long talk with Fran, planning my visit.

Suddenly Fran asked me to hold on, saying someone was knocking at the door. When Fran came back on the phone, she said, "Jack. It's Ray. I have to get off the phone. He's been in an accident and isn't expected to live."

Fran took an early-morning flight out of the small airport near Padre to Dallas, then flew to Minneapolis. She would later learn that Ray had been riding his motorcycle home when a vehicle turned in front of him. Ray tried to lay the bike down but collided with the auto, suffering a severe head injury. Time moved slowly for Fran. Praying, begging, spiraling down to new depths of despair, she nearly lost her mind before she could get to the hospital. *God, I can't take this. Please let Ray recover. Please. Please! I'll do anything.* Guilt flooded back into her mind. Was God punishing her? Was she at fault for this, too? Was God so angry because she wanted to see me that God would take Ray from her as well? At the hospital she made one short call to me, telling me to stay away, not to call her. *I just don't know what else to do. I just know I have to help Ray. If God will let me.*

Two days later, on Father's Day, Ray woke up, recognizing Fran and Lynn at his bedside. "Where's Marlys?" Ray asked. He had forgotten. Once again Fran called me. "Ray woke up. I can't talk now. Jack, I love you, but I don't have time for you now. I have to do everything I can for Ray. Just wait for me to call." Fran's world had crashed. Everything she had she needed to give to Ray, to fight for him and with him to make him recover.

Fran set up housekeeping in Ray's mobile home just across the Stillwater bridge in Houlton, Wisconsin. She drove to the hospital every morning until Ray recovered enough to go home. Lynn now owned Marlys's car and drove herself to her part-time job and to see friends, doing things on her own when she didn't come to the hospital. Jim Wohlenhaus came back to Minnesota, alone this time, to visit Ray and meet with the authorities about the investigation.

In early July, I received a call from Fran. The next day I had dinner with Fran and Ray, then began regular visits to Ray's trailer, as if Fran and I hadn't been apart for even a day. Jim went back to Texas; Greg stayed away. I saw the sun in the sky again, done with the stormy weather of being apart.

Fran's decision to openly spend time with me was the first part of her passage from one life to another during the summer of 1979. We began having dinner out together fairly often, played bridge with her friends, went antique hunting, dancing, listening to country western music. I took Fran to a place where pretty young girls Marlys's age were dancing with good-looking guys Ray's age and wondered why she cried.

In August we stored a load of Fran's things from her house on Trading Post Trail at my home in Forest Lake. Fran had to get on with sorting possessions as part of her divorce. The house remained vacant, since Greg still had his apartment in Stillwater and Fran cared for Ray at his trailer. Fran had help from her friends, packing up what she would be taking, setting aside the things Greg would get. One of her friends cleaned the room where Marlys had been attacked, cutting out the blood-stained carpet, noting there was money—about $100—still on the desk.

Early in the morning of August 17, Ray fainted. He had a high fever, and Fran rushed him to the hospital in St. Paul where his medical records were kept. The doctors put Ray on an antibiotic drip, not sure what was wrong. Fran stood in the waiting room, sat, then paced the hall. After hours of anxiety, she learned that Ray had spinal meningitis. Ray still burned with fever. He would be on the medicine for at least a week, maybe longer.

After the doctors left, Fran sat in a chair in the hallway for a long time. "I can't go on," she said, though no one could hear her. *I've lost my daughter. I can't save my son.* Fear clamped down so hard she couldn't even pray. *I don't know what faith means.* The thought that God had abandoned her struck like a physical blow. Fran walked to a pay telephone and dialed my number. She said, "I can't go on. I don't know if you want this mess of a person I've become, but I'm giving up. I'm turning my life over to you, if you want me."

"Where are you?" I asked.

"At the hospital, but I'm going home. Meet me at the trailer."

I arrived to find her crying. We went to dinner, then to the cemetery, to Marlys's grave.

In September I proposed marriage. Again. Before Marlys was attacked, we had reached the point of trying to figure out where we would live when we were married. As Marlys had pointed out, it wasn't a question of "if." Back in July we talked about some of the practical aspects, but then it was still too soon to say. That summer I truly understood the concept of one day at a time.

But finally Fran said yes. I called her father, who joked that he would give me his permission for her hand, but "you'll have to get her permission for the rest of her." We celebrated by selecting engagement and wedding rings. A week later we went to dinner and I gave her the engagement ring. At the restaurant, Fran said, "I got ready to go out, then waited for your call. I thought perhaps you'd never call me again."

In October I had business in California and asked Fran to fly there with me. We drove to the house where Fran had found refuge when the police sent her out of town. "I want you to see where I went," she said.

More and more, each of us needed to take the other to places with special meaning. Reenacting important experiences helped us transfer good memories and share good feelings. We didn't know it then, but we were beginning a process that would help each of us know each other's former lives, learning about all the children, instinctively doing what we needed to do to blend our families.

We went to Mexico for the day. A photo of the two of us, taken on the beach outside Tijuana, windblown hair and real smiles, has been on display ever since.

Then more bad news struck. On November 5, Patience, the Saint Bernard that had been in the house when Marlys was murdered, died of bloat. After work that day, I picked Fran up, stopping at the cemetery on the way home. Marlys's grave enabled Fran to focus her intense longing on something physical—the cold granite headstone. I stood beside Fran, holding her, feeling her gentle sobbing. I promised Marlys I would always, always take care of her mom. Marlys's body was in the ground, yet we both believed her person to be in heaven. I didn't say the words out loud, but in my mind I vowed, "I promise to take care of your mom, forever, whatever it takes. I promise."

A week later, we found a house that would hold us all: Fran and me, Ray and Lynn, and my three children, JD, Maria, and Shawn. I obtained financing and arranged to move furniture and belongings. Fran was still helping Ray, and she settled my children in school. We even found time to talk again of marriage. Fran said, "I don't have any energy to raise your kids. I'll move in with you, but I'm not sure about a wedding."

"Right now it doesn't matter," I said. "I have to take care of you, no matter what you say."

In December, Crime Stoppers featured Marlys's case on KSTP Radio, which was offering a $10,000 reward. Fran's divorce from Greg became final. Our life was dizzying: we combined two households, enrolled children in new schools, bought and sold vehicles, worked. Less tangibly, we redefined space, merged stepchildren into a reordered hierarchy, and dealt with the emotional shocks each event brought to the embryonic relationships.

On our wedding day, February 6, 1980, ten days after moving into the house, almost nine months after Marlys's murder, I started giving Fran cards with pictures of butterflies. I didn't know any other way to include Marlys in this marriage of which she so clearly and wholeheartedly approved. The simple wedding ceremony merely made legal what had already happened; we became united as a couple, facing a future filled with unknowns. A judge, the two friends who stood up for us, and their spouses made the framework of the rite. Our five remaining children stood by us, unclear about their new roles, uncertain of their place in our hearts.

Slowly our life together began to take shape. We had nearly forty years of life apart from each other, and we vowed we would spend time every day sharing memories. Both of us had kept family photographs, and dividing them for our former spouses became a joint project. Each of us found happiness in seeing the record of the other's children as they grew up. We felt empathy for separate lives in the 1960s and 1970s, each without the other. But always the shadow of the unsolved murder loomed larger than anything else. Before, there was Marlys; after, there was not.

7

The Crime Spree Continues

DONETTE RICO HAD MOVED TO AN APARTMENT in the Minneapolis suburb of Hopkins at the age of seventeen. She told her friends she was smart enough to live on her own. She maintained passing grades at St. Louis Park High School and mostly stayed out of trouble. On October 29, 1979, Donette went to look for her boyfriend, Lee. A rusty red van with an odd-shaped back window pulled up alongside her as she walked through downtown Hopkins. "Wanna ride?" the driver, Joe Ture, asked.

"No thanks," Donette said, not wanting to be distracted from her mission of finding Lee. The van continued to follow her, keeping pace with her as she walked.

"Wanna beer, then?" Ture asked.

Donette stopped walking, considered how showing up in front of Lee with a guy and a beer would be cool, and said, "Yeah."

"Where're you going?" Ture asked, then went on, not waiting for an answer, "My name's Joe. I live in St. Louis Park. You goin' to meet someone? I'm a mechanic. Hey, how come you ain't with a guy?"

"I'm going to the west end," she said, feeling nervous as she realized she might have been wrong to get in the van. The driver seemed creepy.

Ture turned off the main drag and went around into a parking lot, not even a block from where she got in.

"Where you going?" Donette asked.

"I wanna smoke some pot. Don't want to be on the main road."

"Okay, I guess. Fine," she said. The two of them sat in the back of the van, on a bed near a console and cabinets. The curtains in the van had horses printed on them. Ture leaned over, trying to kiss her. Donette pushed at him, then tried to get out the front between the seats. Ture pulled her back, forcing her down flat on her face, her head between the seats. He grabbed her shirt, turning her over and breaking her necklace. "Stop," she shouted. "Get off me. Don't do this." She tried to knee him and scratch him.

Ture slapped her hard once with his open hand, then hit her again. He started to choke her, cutting off her air until she went limp and stopped fighting. Ture pulled down her jeans and underwear and raped her. He pushed her shirt up, exposing her.

When he finished, Ture leaned back, looked at her exposed body, smirking. She remained on the floor, tears running down her cheeks. She struggled to recover her breath. Ture relit his marijuana cigarette. When he put it out, exhaling the last of the smoke, Ture stared hard at Donette. Almost in a rage, he climbed back on her, kissing and touching her, getting himself aroused, then raping her a second time.

Ture dressed himself, then sat on the van floor. "I lied," he said, "about my name. It's Bill. Hey, I'm sorry for what I did." Donette had put her clothes back on and moved to sit on the bed. After a while, saying nothing, both Ture and Donette went back to the front of the van. Ture drove two blocks down the side street where they had parked. "I'm goin' to let you go," he said, showing her a knife. "But don't say nothin' about this. I'll kill you if you do."

Donette got out of the van when Ture stopped, then watched him drive away, noting several letters on the license plate. No longer wanting to find her boyfriend, she started walking. A cab driver she had met at a party saw her and drove her home.

Inside the apartment, Donette sat for a long time alone. Eventually her roommate, Patti Johnson, came home. Donette cried, then opened up. "A guy picked me up, raped me, hit me, choked me till I blacked out."

"We're calling the cops," Patti said.

"I don't know if I can," Donette said. "I just need to think about it." Eventually she cried herself to sleep.

The next morning, Donette's friend Darla convinced her to go to the Hopkins police. Donette called her parents, and her father drove her. She described Joe Ture, his van, and what he had done to her. They took her to Hennepin County Medical Center for a physical exam. Her injuries were photographed.

Officer David Teclaw worked as an investigator for the Hopkins police department. After taking her to the hospital and getting the preliminary medical report, Teclaw met with Donette to take a formal statement. Soon after the meeting, he put out a teletype describing the van, noting the back window and horse-decorated drapes. A day later the van was located; Joe Ture was identified as the owner. Teclaw obtained a search warrant, then seized the van and took Ture into custody.

While the crime lab went over the van, Ture waived his rights to an attorney and talked with Teclaw. "Sure, I gave her a ride," Ture said. "We shared a beer, but I didn't do nothing to her she didn't want done."

"Where are you living, Joe?" Teclaw asked. He had not found the knife Donette spoke of and wanted to search Ture's home.

"I live in my van," Ture said.

"But the van is registered to an address in St. Paul," Teclaw said. "What about that?"

"That's my parents' place. Where I get mail. I don't live with them."

"There is a young woman who says you raped her. What about that?"

"Man, I was too wasted to even know," Ture said. "Is she a fox? I mean, I don't remember a thing."

Although Officer Teclaw took the evidence to the county attorney, he never looked for or talked with the cab driver. He didn't take the photographs of Donette with him to the county attorney, nor did he interview Donette's roommate. The assistant county attorney took the file but did not issue a complaint. Joe Ture was not charged with rape of Donette Rico. He was released and left the area.

In the 1970s, rural Minnesota was a well-spring of tranquillity. St. Cloud, situated on the banks of the still-small upper Mississippi River sixty miles northwest of Minneapolis, was proud to be an embodiment of traditional values as yet unchallenged by the turmoil of war protests and the battle for racial equality that other regions struggled with. City leaders proclaimed it a wonderful place to live, work, and raise a family.

Joan Bierschbach shared a basement apartment in downtown St. Cloud with four other girls, all in their late teens or early twenties. Joanie, as her friends called her, worked at the Stearns County social services office just six blocks away. She walked to work to save the cost of paying for parking. On Monday, November 5, 1979, at 6:30 in the evening, Joanie picked up the telephone, pulled the extra-long extension cord along, went into the bathroom, and called her fiancé, John Fischbach. John had been doing chores in his father's barn in rural Melrose, some twenty-five miles away. John took the call in the milk house. "Hi, John," she said when he came on the line. "I miss you."

"I miss you, too, Joanie. What's up?" John felt some concern, thinking that his fiancée didn't sound ordinary. He would later tell people that he remembered the precise time because he didn't know who would be calling at that time. She never called him. "We're still set for Tuesday, aren't we?" he asked. They had settled into a pleasant routine: Joan went home to Melrose on weekends to visit her family and John. He went to St. Cloud to see her on Tuesdays. "Joanie, what's the echo? The call sounds weird."

"I'm in the bathroom, at my apartment. I wanted to talk but Rhonda is still at the dinner table. I love you, John."

"I love you too, sweetheart."

"I miss you."

"I know. Maybe I shouldn't have gone hunting." John had spent the weekend deer hunting with his sister and her husband.

"No. That's fine. You like to hunt."

"So. Is something the matter?" John asked. "You're not mad because I went?"

"No. It's just, well, I miss you." What Joanie didn't say was that she felt uneasy, that she thought she was being followed. There was this guy she kept seeing. He had approached her once for a date, but she made it clear she didn't want to have anything to do with him. "I'm fine," she said, deciding not to bring up her worries. John might think her silly. "Anyway, John, I'm going to play volleyball tonight. I should go. And I'm meeting Jean at the bowling alley later." Joanie had seen Jean Carls, another of her roommates, earlier in the afternoon and agreed to meet Jean after her volleyball game. Jean thought Joanie seemed happy, as if she had not a care in the world.

After the phone call, Joan changed into a pair of old cords, red tennis shoes, and a blue hooded sweatshirt and said good-bye to Rhonda.

Joanie took pride in her car, a red 1973 four-door Ford Grand Torino. She enjoyed its large motor and bright color. John had helped her find it, checked it out, and went with her when she bought it. There were a few things she didn't like about the car: the glove compartment would pop open, the radio faded in and out on some FM stations. She complained to John about the light in the instrument panel not being bright enough. Shortly after she bought the car, the odometer began to make a metallic clicking noise. John had recently looked under the dash, but he couldn't solve the problem.

When Joanie pulled away from the curb and turned on Division Street, another car came up to her car, almost touching her bumper. She saw the driver in her rearview mirror: a man in his midtwenties with long sideburns. She thought she could see his black leather motorcycle jacket. Joanie had seen him before in the Perkins restaurant just ahead on Division Street. Not wanting to be followed to the volleyball game and the nearly empty parking lot there, Joanie pulled into the Perkins lot. "I'm calling the cops," she said to herself.

The man pulled into the lot behind her and parked right beside her. He cornered her between her car and the entrance to Perkins, walked up to her slowly, then showed her a knife. "Get in the car, bitch," he said, "or this knife is going to be ran in you."

Not knowing what else to do, deathly afraid, Joan Bierschbach got into her car, and slid over to the passenger side when Joe Ture pushed her. He took her keys from her purse, started the car, and drove off, spinning the tires in the wet parking lot. He drove south, out of town toward Monticello.

When Ture drove through slush on the highway, Joanie said, "Don't drive through slush."

Ture backhanded her and shoved her down in the front seat. "You piss me off," he told her. "And shut the hell up," he added when she started praying out loud.

Joanie held on to her crucifix, a gift from John. *If only I had said something to John. Oh, God in heaven help me survive this.* She began reciting the rosary to herself, shivering from fear. "Holy Mary, Mother of God," she whispered, "pray for us sinners, now and at the hour of our death. Our Father," she said as she began a new decade of the rosary.

Ture squirmed as he drove, excited to have a woman captive, agitated by a ticking sound coming from the speedometer. "What's the noise?" he asked. "It's driving me crazy." He continued on Interstate 94 along the Mississippi River, then turned east toward the river on Highway 25 and steered toward a deserted cabin, known as Hart's cabin. Heavy woods to the north ran along the river, and wooded areas and cornfields lay to the south of the cabin.

Ture walked Joanie to a flat area south of the cabin, pointing the knife at her. "Off with your clothes."

"Please. No!" she begged.

"Now," he shouted, waving the knife. When she complied, he punched her, pushed her down, and raped her. While he struggled to complete his assault, Joanie started saying the Lord's Prayer. He hit her again, in the face, but she continued to pray, no longer struggling to defend herself. When Ture finished viciously violating Joan, he started to get up off her. Reflexively, she turned away to cover herself. In an unsatisfied rage, Ture stabbed her in the chest, driving the blade between her ribs, as deep as he could. Soon, but not instantly, Joan Bierschbach died.

Ture calmed down, no longer interested in the dead young woman. He picked up her purse, stuffed her glasses into it, and got back in her car.

On Tuesday evening, John went to Joanie's apartment. Rhonda and Jean asked if Joanie was with him. "No," he said. "I'm supposed to meet her here, like always. I talked to her last night and we made plans." When none of their speculation made sense, John left to look for her. Unable to find her, he decided to call the police, and then he telephoned Lorraine and Ray Bierschbach, her parents. "Come up to her place," he told them. "I need help finding Joanie."

Ronald Buersken, a St. Cloud police officer, responded to John's call, noting John's suspicion of possible foul play. John met him at Joan's apartment, and then her parents arrived. Together they filled out a police report. After Buersken left, John called his brother, who lived in a trailer court on the east side of town, and asked if he could stay overnight. On his way to his brother's trailer at ten o'clock that night, he drove past the Perkins restaurant to make sure Joan's car wasn't there.

The next morning John called a priest and made an appointment to talk to him. En route from his brother's trailer to the church, he noticed Joanie's Grand Torino at the Perkins restaurant. The car sat in the row closest to the street. His hopes soared and he walked through the restaurant but didn't see her. He asked the cashier to see if Joanie was in the bathroom, showing her the high school graduation picture he carried. Then he called Detective Steve Saari and reported finding Joanie's car.

When the patrol officer arrived, he and John looked through the car. The police officer took her purse from the front seat; the driver's door was unlocked, though Joan normally locked her car. John used the keys to open the trunk, fearing the worst. Finding it empty, the officer went through her purse and found a ring John had given her. That seemed odd, because she never took the ring off. Maybe she had put it away because she was going to play volleyball and maybe, he hoped now, she'd hurt her finger at the volleyball game. The car had mud on it, even though Joanie liked to keep it clean. Both her glasses and her contact lenses were in her purse.

Finding the car didn't trigger an investigation: Joan Bierschbach was an adult, and though she had been reported missing, law enforcement officials had to wait three days before beginning a search.

One of the major theories in the investigation into Marlys's death centered on Tom Cartony, a young man who wanted to date Marlys. Another theory had Fran as a probable intended victim, possibly because of her part ownership of the body shop. Fran would pass on to investigators information she remembered about yet another guy who wanted to date Marlys. She gave them names of business associates she found when she looked through her records for anyone Greg might have talked with about his long-range business plans. Fran thought the investigators were following up on these leads. When she asked, they told her they worked on the case every day.

We often discussed the fear that our relationship was in some way related to Marlys's murder. It was not a pleasant thought, even if it was reasonable to ask if our love affair caused somebody to attack Marlys. Could someone have concluded that one of us should not be free to have a different life? Could that person have gone to the house that afternoon in May, striking down Marlys, perhaps thinking he was striking Fran? Many murderers feel justified, however misguided they may be. There is no rational basis to comprehend how someone can commit murder. A deranged mind struck down and killed Marlys.

The investigation remained a daily topic at our new home in Stillwater. On more than one occasion, Fran came home full of frustration at not getting any answers. "I went to see the sheriff," she said after one such visit, putting her car keys in her purse. No longer were they left in the car; no longer was the door to the house unlocked.

"And?" I asked.

"Same thing." She shrugged her shoulders, made a face. "They're working on it every day. So they say. How can they work a case and not follow up the obvious?" She went over her list in her mind. "I asked if they had been to Gene Daniels Restaurant. Richter went the first day after the attack, but he didn't ask them any questions about the Friday-night hassle. Just wanted to see where she worked. Have they talked to Jackie about Sunday night at the place? No. She's scared. 'So what?' I said to them." Fran didn't have to add that she herself knew that fear.

Both of us felt confused because efforts to solve the crime were going nowhere. Our suspicions were deep and divisive, partly because our imaginations and the police investigation scattered over a dozen possible suspects. Marlys's closest friends also felt the fear of the unsolved crime and withdrew from contact with Fran. The girlfriends continued to work at the small restaurant where Marlys had worked, but no connection was made between that place and the investigation into Marlys's murder. Everywhere Fran went in the once-pleasant St. Croix River Valley, places and people reminded her of her daughter. Marlys's killer still roamed free out there, unknown. Simple living no longer seemed possible for our scrambled family.

In February 1980 we had an open house to celebrate our marriage, then drove east on business. We stopped to visit my parents in Chicago, took care of my work in Philadelphia, then drove south to see Fran's parents in Richmond. We used wedding-gift money to buy an antique china cupboard.

We drove back through the Virginia mountains and past Purdue University, where I went to college, sharing memories and places with each other. We were going through the motions of acting normal and getting on with life.

Part II

Grief

8

The First Exile

I CONTINUED TO WORK in the patent law department of a major corporation in Minneapolis. Management gave me more understanding, even compassion, than anyone might have expected from the corporate world. There was nothing wrong with the work or the job. One day, however, I brought home news of a position within the company opening up in Philadelphia. "There's an opportunity to move," I said.

At first Fran said she couldn't leave Marlys behind, even in the grave. Then she began to talk about her fears. "I go out of my way so I won't drive past the body shop," she said. "That's so dumb."

"Not dumb," I said. "There isn't any place that's not filled with memories."

"I like the memories. It's just that I'm afraid."

"Me, too," I said. "After Marlys was attacked, when I went jogging I used to wonder if someone would run their car into me."

"Someone might," she said. After Fran and I talked about it for a few days, she made a decision. "I'll go to Philadelphia if you want. In fact, I don't know how I can stay here." The next day I asked to be considered for the transfer, and Fran and I began to think about what a long-distance move would mean.

Fran's two children, nearly adult now, didn't like the idea but weren't quite ready to be on their own, especially Ray, who was still recovering from his accident. Lynn wanted to graduate from Stillwater High. My three children had just been uprooted, changed schools in midyear, found new friends and activities, and spent time regularly with their mom. What right did I have now to tell them they were going to move halfway across the continent?

Those were hard questions to deal with in an inverted world where a home had become a murder scene. The reason Fran and I finally decided to leave was simple: life elsewhere, no matter how different from our recent past, might at least be free from fear. We would move even if I didn't get the transfer. We needed a sanctuary. We were running away because we were unable to fight.

It's surprisingly easy to accomplish a cross-country move. I called a "headhunter" employment agency, made a connection with another company in Philadelphia, visited the corporate offices, and received an offer on the spot. A day later I accepted, then we made plans to find a new house. None of the children were speaking to us. Why should they? These two parents were a disaster.

In early December 1980, our caravan of vehicles left Minnesota, loaded with Saint Bernards and Fran's first Dandie Dinmont terrier, her plants and bulbs, and our five children plus two more young adults who came along for the ride. More than twelve hundred miles later, we arrived two days ahead of the moving vans, ready to take possession of a home in Paoli, Pennsylvania, that we had acquired on a lease and purchase agreement. Paoli, at the end of an area of suburban Philadelphia called the Main Line because it developed along the main route of the Pennsylvania Railroad when it first moved west, is famous for a massacre in the 1700s and for being the home of Revolutionary War General "Mad Anthony" Wayne. Both Fran and I thought the three-story English Tudor house would be a refuge where going on with life without Marlys might be possible.

We had good intentions. We fixed up a bedroom for each of the kids. I bought a new suit and went to work on the commuter train. We invited friends we knew from raising Saint Bernards to watch the Super Bowl with us. We went to school conferences, started attending church, did all the things that might bring life into focus. I took Fran to nearby places I had visited on business in earlier years. Our first anniversary was a happy day. The kids gave us nice presents and we retreated into the master bedroom suite. The house was old and needed repair, but it represented a vision that the future might turn out to be good, or at least not tragic.

Mother's Day came on May 10 that year, a double reminder of our loss. After that, things started to unravel. First one then another of my children rebelled at new discipline, less attention, more competition for affection. We couldn't keep the English Tudor because interest rates were skyrocketing and we still hadn't sold the house in Minnesota. Ray and his girlfriend moved into Philadelphia. Lynn left for Minnesota to stay with a girlfriend to finish high school with her class. We drove out for her graduation and visited friends. Though Fran saw her "lunch bunch," it wasn't the same anymore. She wanted to talk about Marlys, not get on with life as the girls expected.

And the sheriff had no news about the investigation.

When we returned to Pennsylvania, we moved to a more affordable house in Malvern, the next town west. A few weeks later the well died. I lamented that I certainly wasn't keeping my promise to Marlys to take care of her mother, whatever that means when two out-of-orbit planets spin in space, no longer in celestial harmony.

Our life was painful, with debt, anxiety, and worry about family. Fran had taken a job so we would qualify for the onerous 15 percent interest rate on our mortgage. She took care of everyone's needs but her own. In that crowd, she was alone with her memories, not able to say Marlys's name without crying, yet closing up when anyone tried to ask about her pain. We were carrying on as though there wasn't anything different about being the mother and stepfather of a murder victim. We didn't know one could talk about birthdays and death days, certainly not realizing how normal remembering is and how paralyzing it is to even think of forgetting.

While we struggled to regain our balance, in exile from our dreams of living and loving in Minnesota, Joe Ture remained free. His reign of terror continued, though we were not yet aware of what other victims would suffer.

Rosemary Kurzhal, a seventeen-year-old runaway, was walking along White Bear Avenue in St. Paul when Joe Ture pulled up on his motorcycle. "Wanna ride?" Ture asked.

"Sure," Rosemary said, not having anyplace to go. She got on the back of the bike, holding on to Ture's waist. He drove to an apartment complex, then pulled up in front of a garage. "What's this?" she said.

"I live here. Some buddies live in the apartment there," Ture pointed, "and I stay here. I'll show you," he said, opening the door. He led her into the garage. "Take off your clothes," Ture said.

"No."

Ture grabbed Rosemary, pushed her down, pinned her legs, and undressed her. Though she tried to get away, slapped him, pushed him, Ture was too strong, and he raped her. When he finished, Ture got up, pointed to her clothes, and said, "We're going out. Me and you, together."

"Just leave me here," she answered, getting dressed. "You already got what you wanted. Let me go."

"No. You're coming with me," he said, grabbing her, pushing her shirttails into her pants. Scared, degraded, feeling hopeless, she went with him. Ture drove to Dow Auto, where he had been working. Keeping Rosemary at his side, Ture then took her to a bar, T. R. Potts. Ture ordered a drink for himself, and when he went into the bathroom, Rosemary had a chance to call for help.

Moments later, a West St. Paul police officer arrived at the bar. Rosemary met him outside. "There's a guy in there who raped me," she said. She gave a false name, not wanting to be found out as a runaway.

The officer looked her over, trying to see some evidence of violence to support her allegations. "Where did he rape you?" he asked. "Not here?"

"No," Rosemary said. "Look. I just want to get away from him."

"Well, are you all right?"

"I guess so. I just want to leave." Rosemary could see the officer didn't really believe her, and she would have no way of making the cop believe her accusations against Ture.

"Okay," the officer said, "I'll take you where you want to go. Do you want to go to the hospital, be checked out?"

"No," she said. "Just get me out of here. You can take me to a friend's house." She gave the officer an address in St. Paul.

The officer never went into the bar to have a look at the alleged rapist.

The next day, still in fear and shame, still not willing to go back home to her parents, Rosemary took another walk, to visit another friend. To her shock and surprise, Ture pulled up again, got off his motorcycle, and grabbed her. "You're going with me again," he said, pulling on her arm.

Numb with fear, Rosemary said nothing, just followed along, trying to avoid more violence. Ture raped her again, then locked her in the garage, where she spent the night alone.

The next morning he came back and made her carry some of his possessions when he moved to a different garage. After they finished, he made her get on his motorcycle for another errand. Rosemary felt safest when Ture treated her like a girl-friend, including her in his activities. She feared for her life when he became aroused, as though he had to prove something by forcing himself on her. They rode into St. Paul, where Ture pulled into a Country Kitchen parking lot. He pulled through the parking lot to the back near a grove of trees mostly obscuring a tractor trailer. Thinking this was an opportunity to get free, Rosemary jumped off the bike when he stopped by the trailer. She screamed for help and ran toward the restaurant but Ture moved faster, grabbing her by the back of her shirt. He pulled her into the trailer and forced her to disrobe again.

"Don't do this," she begged. "You told me you wouldn't do this to me anymore." Rosemary hit at him and tried to kick him.

"Well, I'm going to do it one more time." And he did. "I could kill you if I wanted to," Ture said, getting up off her. "Remember that." He tossed her clothes to her.

Back once again on the motorcycle behind Joe Ture, Rosemary began to despair. They stopped at Stockmen's Truck Stop, and Ture let her go to the women's room.

Rosemary sought help from a woman in the rest room. "I'm being kept by this guy. He keeps raping me. I can't get away."

The woman saw her desperation and walked with her to Ture. "Let me go," Rosemary said to him.

"Oh, go. Go ahead, go," he replied.

The next day Rosemary met a trucker who took her to the East Coast. In time, she hitchhiked back to Minnesota and finally went back home to her parents.

On September 26, 1980, Ture quit work at Rood Tool at about 7:30 p.m. It was time to prowl again.

Tomi Willems lived in South St. Paul and worked at a bank in downtown St. Paul. At about 8:30 p.m., on her way to her sister's house, she stopped at a 7-Eleven. After leaving the store, Tomi noticed a car following closely, maybe only two feet behind her, with its bright lights on, though only one worked. At a stop sign, the car following her hit her from behind, more like a push, not enough to damage either car. She thought she could see a lone male—Joe Ture, it turned out—and from his expression she thought he had hit her deliberately.

The driver backed up, screeching his tires, then pulled alongside her car. He got out of his car and tried to get into hers. Tomi quickly drove off. Ture drove on the wrong side of the road to pass her, then pulled in front of her and stopped his car. She tried to drive to Ture's right, then to the left, but Ture blocked her. She laid on the horn; luckily, another car was coming up behind her. Ture drove off and she followed him until he turned toward the Signal Hills Shopping Center. The car was a dark-colored older-model station wagon with considerable rust. When Ture turned, Tomi drove away as fast as she could, running a stop sign, then called her sister and mother to come for her. Crying, she felt too upset to drive further. Ture continued to search for a victim.

Donald and Bonnie Edwards lived in West St. Paul. He worked as a chemical engineer at 3M and she worked at the Wilder Foundation in St. Paul. Their daughter Diane lived with them; she had lived on campus during her first year at the University of Minnesota and planned to live at home during her sophomore year. Diane worked at a Perkins restaurant in West St. Paul, nine blocks from her home. She dated a young man named Mark Johnson, who picked her up on Thursday, September 25, after she finished her regular shift at Perkins. They went to the West Fargo Lounge, then to Johnson's residence, where they stayed until 4:30 a.m.

On Friday, September 26, Bonnie Edwards took a day off work to shop with her daughter before Diane went to work. They were getting ready for the new school year. Diane left for work about 4:00, walking as she usually did. She wore the orange and tan Perkins uniform and carried a white sweater. When her shift ended, she served herself a fried chicken dinner with french fries and told the assistant manager good-bye.

Down the block, fifteen-year-old Kelly Christopherson had been hanging out with three friends: Carrie Christenson, Linda Gross, and Laurie Cline. They had gone to Signal Hills Shopping Center, a small mall in West St. Paul. At about 9:00 p.m., the girls left the shopping center and began walking to McDonald's, two blocks south. When they walked through the parking lot, a car drove past and went around them. The driver honked at the girls. The car, a dark-colored station wagon, didn't have a light on the license plate.

The girls watched the car because one of them noticed that the driver, a man, was alone in the car. Carrie said, "Somebody is going to get a hard time," prompting Kelly to try to get a better look at the car. The station wagon pulled up behind Diane Edwards as she walked home. Kelly noticed her blond hair when the headlights lit her up. The driver seemed to go around Diane. Kelly turned away. Carrie also saw the car drive onto the sidewalk so the driver's side door was next to Diane. The door opened, and the driver got partway out and grabbed Diane, who started screaming.

Kelly looked back when she heard the scream. "Did that just happen?" she asked. They watched Diane struggle, unable to get free. The four girls started to run toward the car, which drove off when they got close. They hurried to McDonald's and asked the staff to call the police.

At that same time, Kathryn Dahn, who lived nearby, sat in a friend's car while her friend and Dahn's daughter went into the Laundromat behind the Signal Hills Shopping Center. Dahn relaxed in the driver's seat, watching the world go by. Sitting sideways toward the inside of the car, she noticed a car headed toward her, going much slower than the average traffic. She couldn't see any other cars on the road. When the car reached a point just behind her, she saw Diane, almost as if she appeared out of nowhere. Diane and the driver talked briefly, then he got out and picked her up and threw her into the car, into the driver's side. Diane was screaming. For whatever

reason, Dahn didn't report the abduction but simply watched
Joe Ture drive away.

At about 9:10, a West St. Paul police dispatcher called the
Edwards home, saying that four teenage girls had seen someone in a Perkins uniform whom the police believed was Diane
being grabbed and thrown into a station wagon. Don went to
Perkins, and learned that Diane had gotten off work at about
8:30, ate a meal, then left to walk home at a few minutes
before 9:00.

Ture sped off with Diane Edwards in his 1970 brown Ford
station wagon, forcing her down on the front seat. After about
six blocks, he stopped and tied her hands behind her back with
clothesline rope he had already tied in a hangman's knot. Then
he shoved a towel in her mouth, to stop her from screaming
and hollering. Ture drove through St. Paul to Interstate 694,
then toward Elk River.

North out of Elk River about six miles, Ture turned into
a secluded area, pulled Diane out of the car, and raped her.
Diane screamed, and Ture stabbed her three times: below her
waist, just above her waist, and then just below her neck. He
dragged her out of the car and down an embankment, then
raped her dead or dying body. Then he folded her clothes
neatly and placed them next to her, putting her shoes on top
of the pile.

Up in Elk River, Richard Bolin had a day off from college on
October 9, 1980, and decided to go hunting in the rural area
near his home. His parents owned ten acres; to the north the
Girl Scouts owned 2,500 acres and to the east were 5,000 acres
owned by a Minneapolis-based company. There were no homes
on any of this property. Richard walked down a dirt road,
around the duck-hunting pond, back into the Girl Scouts
property. He saw a woman's purse lying three feet off the side
of the road and picked it up. The small dark-blue purse held a
wallet and a checkbook.

Thinking it might be important, Richard went home and showed the purse to his mother. Mrs. Bolin called the phone number on the checks, reaching Don Edwards. "I've found a purse with a wallet and checkbook," she said. "Diane Edwards is the name printed on the checks, and I'm calling because she may have lost it."

"What's your telephone number?" Don Edwards asked. He wrote it down and said, "Just wait right there, at your home."

Two minutes later, the Bolins' telephone rang, and Mrs. Bolin talked to a police officer who told her not to touch anything and that they would be at her home soon.

When Sergeant Bauerfeld and Detective William Cook of the West St. Paul police arrived, they confirmed that the purse belonged to Diane Edwards. Richard and his mother drove to the place where he had found the purse, closely followed by the officers. He pointed to where the purse had been, and Cook noticed a pair of eyeglasses with one lens missing; he found the other lens nearby. Cook photographed the objects and put them in the trunk of the squad car. They called the Sherburne County sheriff's office, which had jurisdiction here, then waited for them to arrive.

Sheriff Chet Gunner, Chief Deputy David Hofstad, and other deputies soon arrived. Quickly the search began. A state Highway Patrol helicopter and two helicopters from local television stations began sweeping the area. Hofstad ordered a deputy to be put in each of the three choppers after determining that the news-helicopter pilots were eager to cooperate. Within five minutes, one of the airborne deputies called Hofstad on a walkie-talkie.

"We've spotted something," he said. "Drive up the dirt road and stop when I tell you."

Hofstad followed the deputy's directions, then got out of the car to walk down the bank. "I don't see anything," he said to the deputy, using his walkie-talkie.

"Take a few steps left. To your left." Hofstad gasped when he saw a young woman lying on her stomach. Her legs were spread apart, her hands were folded, and her head was down. Clothing was piled, with tennis shoes on top, near her arm. Hofstad reached down, touching her arm to be sure there was no life, looked around without moving, then went back up the bank and gave orders to tape off the scene. He called for the county attorney and the coroner, then waited.

When the Sherburne County coroner arrived, he asked Cook to call the Ramsey County medical examiner's office and arranged to have Dr. Michael McGee flown to the scene in a Highway Patrol helicopter. After taking photographs and making an initial examination, discovering stab wounds, Dr. McGee had Diane transported to St. Paul.

9

Out of His Own Mouth

THE INVESTIGATION into Diane Edwards's abduction
and murder began immediately, based in Sherburne
County because Minnesota law gives jurisdiction to the county
where a crime is committed. Dr. McGee felt certain that Diane
Edwards had been killed at the scene, after being raped and
beaten. Chief Deputy David Hofstad coordinated the efforts
of his Sherburne County deputies with help from both the
Minnesota Bureau of Criminal Apprehension and the West
St. Paul police investigators. At first there were no suspects,
and none of the crime scene analysis yielded any clues.

When West St. Paul Detective Jeffrey Batzel reported for
duty on September 27, he noticed the missing person report
and began working the case. His team generated a great deal
of publicity through the media. Don Edwards's employer, the
3M company, prepared a flyer with Diane's photograph and
a composite drawing made from descriptions offered by Kelly
Christopherson, Carrie Christenson, Linda Gross, and Laurie
Cline, though none of the girls got a good look at the driver.

As the investigation proceeded, Ture continued his crime
spree, seemingly invisible to authorities, not at all connected
to the abduction and murder of Diane Edwards. At least he
thought he was safe. He put his car, a brown station wagon,
through an automobile crusher at a scrap yard. On October 19,
Ture picked up and raped Lisa Wilke. On October 25, Ture

assaulted and raped Crystal Solie, who went to the police and identified Ture from a photo lineup. Then things started to unravel. Ture was arrested on October 30 and charged with two counts of rape. The two women were prepared to testify against him. Ture now sat in the Hennepin County jail.

During the Diane Edwards investigation, a White Bear Lake police officer told Batzel he knew about a man who had been hanging around a Perkins restaurant in White Bear Lake, bothering some of the waitresses. Now having a suspect, Batzel and his working partner, Dakota County sheriff's department Lieutenant Richard Hudella, began finding out all they could about Joseph Donald Ture Jr.

Rosemary Kurzhal's name surfaced as one of the more than four hundred people the investigators interviewed in the case. Batzel tracked down Rosemary's father, who met with the investigators at his house. After a brief conversation, Batzel and Stearns County sheriff's department Detective Lou Leland took Rosemary to the West St. Paul police department to take a formal statement. Rosemary described the motorcycle, the garages, the rapes, and her escape. She confirmed that she had left town the day of the abduction of Diane Edwards. She gave Batzel the name of the truck driver who drove her east, who later confirmed her story. Joe Ture now faced a third count of rape.

With this information and with Ture in the Hennepin County jail, Batzel and Hudella went to visit their suspect. The conversation was the first of several, none of which helped the case.

Archie Sonenstahl, a detective in the Hennepin County sheriff's department, also had conversations with Ture. On April 29, 1981, a call came from the jail to the criminal division, where Sonenstahl worked, saying that Ture wanted to talk to the sheriff. Because he was the on-call detective, Sonenstahl went to Ture's cell to find out what he wanted. Ture complained that the jailers and other inmates were harassing him because he was accused of being a rapist. Though Sonenstahl had not been involved in the Diane Edwards case, he knew that Ture had been connected to the place where Diane disappeared. Sonenstahl gave Ture his card and left, saying, "Call me if you have any more problems."

"I might," Ture said. "Nobody ever cares about me." Ten days later Ture called Sonenstahl, and they met again on May 11. Ture moaned about having been found guilty of the three rape charges. "I don't wanna go to the Stillwater prison. I wanna safer place."

"I'll see what I can do," Sonenstahl said.

"Maybe I need treatment," Ture said.

"Maybe you do—the rapes and all."

"If I was to cooperate on the Edwards case, do you think I could get some treatment? In exchange?"

"I can't say," Sonenstahl answered. "It depends on the type of treatment and the amount of cooperation you give." Sonenstahl gave Ture a Miranda warning, making sure he was aware of his rights as a suspect. Ture waived his right to counsel, then made a detailed confession to the abduction and murder of Diane Edwards. Sonenstahl then left and came back with Detective Batzel; they tape-recorded a second confession, again after a Miranda warning.

Turning the recorder off, Sonenstahl asked about the remote location, surprisingly far from West St. Paul. "How in hell did you ever find that spot way out there in the boonies?"

"I knew the spot," Ture replied, "because I snowmobiled out there a few times."

Sonenstahl called Chief Deputy David Hofstad in Sherburne County to inform him of the confession. The two decided to see if Ture would show them the route he took with Diane Edwards. When Ture agreed, Sonenstahl got a court order releasing Ture from jail into Sonenstahl's custody. That afternoon, riding in Hofstad's squad car, Sonenstahl and Ture sat in the back seat while Hofstad drove and Hennepin County

Captain Chuck Ostlund rode in front. Ture directed them to the intersection where he bumped Tomi Willems, then past the Signal Hills Shopping Center, identified where the four girls were standing, then where he grabbed Diane.

On the way, Ture pointed out an adult bookstore: "It's a good place to pick up hookers," he said. He continued to direct the ride, instructing Hofstad when to turn. Finally they reached the dirt road where Diane had been found. "Stop right here," Ture said. "This is where it happened."

"Can you show me the spot?" Hofstad asked.

"I can," Ture replied.

Sonenstahl and Hofstad got out of the car while Ostlund stayed with Ture in the car. Hofstad told Sonenstahl where he found Diane's body, without pointing. Then they went back to the squad car.

"Joe," Sonenstahl said, "can you show us exactly where?"

"Sure." When Ture got out of the car, he walked ten feet or so, then down the sloping embankment while the three officers stayed up on the road. Ture walked over to a little tree and said, "There's the woods I told you about."

"Fine," Sonenstahl said.

"I think it was right about—right about here." Ture stopped, then urinated on the ground.

Sonenstahl told Ture he had gotten within four feet of the actual spot. Ture just smiled. When they turned the car around, Ture pointed out the window. "I think I threw the glasses and the purse right about here somewhere." The next day Ture was transported to the Sherburne County jail. Soon he would go to trial for first-degree murder of Diane Edwards.

During the trial, a convicted felon, Toby Krominga, was brought to Ture's Sherburne County cell block. The two inmates didn't say much before lockdown, at about 10 p.m., when each was locked into his own cell. The next morning, the jailer woke the two men, opening up the individual cells to the central area of the cell block, and set breakfast on the table. Ture reached across the table and took Krominga's coffee. "You ain't taking my coffee," Krominga said.

"I took it," Ture said. Krominga stood up and punched Ture, who fell backward without trying to fight back.

Later in the morning, Ture changed the channel on the television, then told Krominga, "I watch sports. I watch what I want to watch."

In reply, Krominga punched Ture again. They fought for a moment, then Ture gave up and went to his cell. At lunch, Ture seemed more mellow, even offering his coffee to Krominga. After the conflict they coexisted but did not talk about their criminal records. Getting along and minding one's own business defined normal jail and prison conduct.

One day, Ture opened the subject of his crimes. "I'm on trial," Ture said, "for murder. I been carrying a Bible to courts. You think that impresses the jury?"

"I don't think so," Krominga said.

"Well, what if they thought I was crazy?"

"That won't impress them, either."

"Naw, I mean, what would people think if I killed a bunch of people?"

"I'd think you were nuts," Krominga said.

"Well, I gotta do something. This trial is going bad. Real bad." After the evidence came in on his identifying the place where Diane was found, Ture told Krominga, "I should have buried the bitch."

Krominga and Ture worked out a plan: Ture would write a letter confessing to his crimes. Krominga had access to writing materials because he had been sentenced to a state prison, giving him greater property rights than someone held in a county jail. Jailer Leon Dehen brought him the materials, including several ballpoint pens of different makes. Krominga wanted to do the writing as a diversion to break the monotony of sitting in a cell block all day.

Krominga had been convicted of a number of felonies, some involving confidence schemes. He would tell you that you couldn't trust him, almost as if he dared you to try. Krominga told Ture that the confession would be sent to the judge to show Ture's mental state, but he had other plans as well. He contacted the woman he called his wife, Maureen Dickenson, who kept in contact with Thomas Matthews, a reporter Krominga knew.

Ture talked about the murder of Alice Huling and her three children. He bragged about being arrested and getting out, even told Krominga that if they had asked him back in 1978 when they arrested him, he would have confessed. In all, Krominga wrote out four yellow legal pages of details on the Hulings, including killing the chickens and then coming back to commit the murders. Though he didn't show any emotion, Krominga reacted to Ture's statement that he shot Alice to disable her, told her he was going to kill her children, then came back down to finish her off. This, in Krominga's mind, justified sending the confessions to the press. Ture also told Krominga about killing Marlys, adding three pages to the document.

Krominga had written out the confessions several times, making a final draft more than a week after they began the project to keep Ture from doing hard time. Halfway through the last draft, Krominga changed pens. Once the seven pages were complete, Krominga had Dehen hand them to Ture, who read them and signed them. In a blank space Krominga left on the page, Ture drew in the weapon he used to kill Marlys.

On her next visit to the prison, Dickenson got the written confession from Krominga and took it to Matthews. Television station KSTP broke the story. Within a day, the news would be broadcast on every news show in Minnesota. The reporters flocked to Washington County to quiz Sheriff Jim Trudeau and Undersheriff Ken Boyden.

David Hofstad had been in the Sherburne County sheriff's department for almost nine years, moving up to acting sheriff for a short time, then transferred to the county attorney's office. Hofstad worked in the prosecutor's office, assigned directly to the case against Joe Ture for the murder of Diane Edwards. During the trial, County Attorney John McGibbon, Hofstad, and others prosecuting the case would gather in the Sherburne County law library. Ture, as is standard procedure, remained in the Sherburne County jail except when deputies escorted him to the courtroom. The judge appointed public defender Bruce Douglas to represent Ture, since Ture had no assets. Occasionally Hofstad would see Douglas in the library or in the halls, where they had social conversations.

Hofstad spent Thanksgiving weekend 1981 with his parents and his brother's family. During dinner, he got a telephone call from Duane Margison, a KSTP cameraman. "David," Margison said, "have you ever talked to Ture?"

"I have some time ago," Hofstad replied, "but not lately. Why?"

"Did he ever mention anything about chickens? It has to do with the Huling case."

"I've never heard anything about it," Hofstad said.

"Well," Margison said, "next time you can talk to him, ask him about that. And, while you're talking to him, ask him about the Wohlenhaus girl in Afton."

After he hung up, Hofstad complained to his family about never having peace in his job. "Give me a break," he said to his father. "Those guys can't ever leave me alone. I have no idea how they got this telephone number."

"I'm in the phone book, son," his father said.

The Monday after the holiday, Hofstad went to his boss, who said, "Yeah, it can't hurt anything. But remember, you got to talk to Bruce before you go down there." As Hofstad started to leave, McGibbon added, "And make sure you read him his rights."

Later, in the hallway by the courtroom, Hofstad approached Ture's lawyer. "Bruce," Hofstad said, "could I talk to Joe Ture?"

"As long as you don't talk to him about Diane Edwards, you can talk to him. What's he done now?"

"I don't know. I just want to ask him some things."

"I've told him not to talk to anyone, but I can't control what he does."

"Thanks, Bruce," Hofstad said. "He's talked to some other investigators already."

"I know, Dave. But nothing about Edwards."

Hofstad called down to the jail and told the jailer on duty to bring Ture to the small conference room just off the jail dispatcher's office. Hofstad had interviewed Ture there many times.

When Hofstad came into the room, Ture was waiting for him. Hofstad recited the Miranda warning, then said, "Joe, are you willing to talk to me today?"

"No paper, no pencil," Ture said, "and I will talk to you about anything you want to talk about."

Hofstad put his yellow legal pad aside and sat down at the table with Ture. "Joe, you know, up in St. Cloud, there was that Huling thing."

"So?"

"So, Joe, were there any chickens on that?"

"How should I know?" Ture answered.

Not knowing anything more than what the cameraman had said, Hofstad let the subject drop. "Okay. Say, Joe, did you know that Wohlenhaus girl over in Afton?"

"Yeah. I knew her," Ture said. "I wanted to date her, to talk to her, so I went to her house and she wasn't home yet. I went in the house and waited."

"What happened then?" Hofstad asked.

"We talked and we argued, and then I killed her."

"Killed her? How?"

"I used a hatchet," Ture said, smirking.

"You killed her? Why?" Ture turned away from Hofstad and refused to answer any other questions. Even when

Hofstad tried to talk about other things, Ture remained silent, so Hofstad had Ture taken back to his cell.

Hofstad called the Washington County sheriff's office, identified himself, and told the receptionist that he wanted to talk to somebody about the Wohlenhaus murder case. He was told that nobody was available, so he left a message: Joe Ture had just told him that he had killed the girl. Would somebody get back to him?

We heard about the confession when a reporter called Fran. An hour later, Washington County Undersheriff Ken Boyden called to tell us the same news. Fran's ex-husband, Greg Loux, called during the broadcast and put the telephone next to the television. After we listened to the confession, in which Ture claimed to have worked for Greg, Greg told Fran that Ture had never worked for him. "I don't know if the rest is true, but he never worked for me," Greg said.

Boyden mailed a copy of the confession to Fran, asking her to go over every word. "What is true and what is not?" he asked. The three handwritten pages we saw that related to Marlys's murder, with typos and all, read:

> My name is Joseph Ture. I am making this second state-
> ment in hopes of getting to St. Peter State Hospital for treat-
> ment. I am making this statement of my own will, I am not
> being pressured or forced into making this statement. I am
> aware of the fact that I could be in a lot of trouble for making
> this statement. I am again having Toby Krominga write it
> for me while I tell him what to put down, because he spells
> better than I do.
>
> In this statement I want to talk about the Marlys
> Wholhouse murder. I'm not sure of the spelling of her name.
> I worked for her Dad at his Body Shop, Greg's body shop.
> I was a mechanic, and he paid me in cash for tax reason's we
> both made out. I also went to Milwaukee Wisconsin a few
> times to pick up car's for Greg, he's running a chop shop. One

day he had an argument with his wife, and afterwards he
said he would pay a lot to get rid of that bitch. So I decided
to do that, and after, I got rid of her I was going to go to
Greg for a bunch of money. And get out of the state. I went
to the house. I knew where it was because I was there before
to pick up money from Greg. To get there I went up a steep
hill and took the right fork, to get to the Wholehouse. I
pulled into the driveway. I was driving a 1967 Mustang white
hard top. The dog a St. Bernard was outside raising hell. So
I stayed in the car waiting for Mrs. Wholenhouse to come
out. No one came out, and I was about to leave when Marlys
Wholenhouse showed up. She's a little shit. About 5'6" with
strawberry blond hair. She was wearing jeans, I can't remember what color blouse. I asked her where her mother was. She
said working. I told Marlys who I was, and that I wanted to
see her mother. I knew Marlys a little, and she knew of me.
We both bought drugs at Nybo's restaurant. I asked her if
she wanted to smoke a joint. And she said OK. We went into
the house at the back door. The dog looked like he wanted
a piece of me. So I asked Marlys' to lock him up somewhere
because he scared me. She took him to her bedroom. I waited
inside the back door by her Dad's office. When Marlys came
back we went down a couple of steps to the basement. The
house is a split level. We went to the rec room and smoked
a joint. I told her I would get her some real good dope for a
piece of ass. She said hell no, I wouldn't go to bed with you.
So I figured I needed a weapon to convince her of the idea.
So I told her my car wouldn't start. And I needed some tools.
She pointed to where the storeroom was and said look in
there. So I went to the store room, and found a hatchet on a
work bench [sketch of hatchet]. I went back to the storeroom
with the hatchet, and told Marlys, I wanted some pussy. She
said bug off, and to get the hell out of the house. I freaked
and hit her 3 or 4 times in the head with the hatchet. I heard
the dog going crazy up stairs so I left in a hurry. On my way

I was going to take a C.B. radio from the office but decided not to. Because I never take anything that will tie me to the crime. I was going to drive away real slow without attracting attention, but when I got to the fork of the road, I saw some little bitch looking at me, so I spun gravel and got the hell out of there. I threw the hatchet off a bridge in South St. Paul, by the Concord St. Exit, going west across the bridge. Then I went to MPLS. on Hennipen Ave. And got a nigger whore and got laid. I don't want to talk about this any more, so end of statement.

signed: Joseph Ture 12/15/81

witness: Toby Krominga 12/15/81

"Oh, God," Fran said, handing the paper to me. "Could this really be true?"

"Some of it is," I said after reading it. "Do you want to go over it together? Some of it doesn't make sense, but maybe there is information only someone at the scene would know."

"I sure do," she said, sitting at the kitchen table. "Boyden's note says for me to do that."

I got a legal pad to make notes while Fran waited, unhappy with the lies she had read about Marlys. When I came back she took the pad. "You read it out loud," she said, "one sentence at a time. I'll write some comments."

We began, line by line. "Okay. He says he worked for Greg." And Greg denies it.

"That's possible, at least in 1979. Remember, I didn't go to the shop except when I had to."

"He says he was a mechanic and Greg paid him in cash for tax reasons."

"Well, again, I don't know."

"Did he go to Milwaukee to pick up cars?"

"That's possible, especially in March when Ray was in Texas."

A lot of the statement was familiar to both of us, bringing

back a reality that had been burned into our minds. "Look at the next sentence," I said. "He says he knew Marlys and she knew 'of' him."

"I see the distinction," Fran said, "like he could have been the one who hassled her at Gene Daniels. If he did talk to Marlys, he could have said he drove for somebody. He might have talked his way into her confidence with stories about driving to Milwaukee. She didn't know about the business."

"He says Marlys took the dog to her bedroom."

"That's not where Patience was. But it would have been easy to mix up my bedroom and Marlys's. And there wasn't an office on the upper level. Plus, the only CB was the base unit in the kitchen-dining area at the back door. Wait a minute," Fran added, thinking about the house. "It is possible the CB out of my car was on the ledge in the rec room by the basement door."

"I remember hatchets," I said.

"The hatchet on the ledge near the side door in the rec room has not been accounted for. At one time there was one on the ledge by that door, as Greg and his sons used all three hatchets to chop wood before they moved out in April. I don't recall whether the hatchet was still there or not, but I do remember seeing a couple of hatchets outside on a stump we used for a chopping block."

"So he might be telling the truth about the murder weapon. What about the storeroom?"

"I distinctly remember when I came home to find Marlys, the back room that we called the storage room was open and I definitely recall that it was closed when I left the house. I kept it shut because I had been packing and the room was a mess. If Marlys was surprised in the den office area, he would have been hiding in there."

"This could be the answer, Fran." Both of us could see how some pieces of the puzzle fit where we expected; others had no shape we could recognize.

Two days went by, and then the bubble burst. Ture had recanted his confession, said he only did it to get sentenced to an easier prison, denied even having been in Afton. He also had an alibi. He was at work, he claimed, and couldn't have committed the crime. An investigator who checked records at the Ford factory in St. Paul learned that Joseph Donald Ture had been at work when Marlys was attacked. He appeared to be cleared. Our hopes were crushed.

Fran and I went back to Minnesota some months later and met with Washington County investigators for an update. Fran went over the confession again, checking facts and noting statements where she had a problem, mostly in the conversation Ture said he had with Marlys. She was outraged at the things Ture said about her daughter. But because the alibi seemed to hold up, Boyden and the others told Fran that their conclusion was that Ture had fabricated the story. It was no use going down this path any longer. The matter was dropped.

10

If I Can't Have Marlys Back

*I*F IT WASN'T THIS PERSON, a murderer convicted of killing Diane Edwards, a serial killer perhaps, then who was it? Was Marlys the victim of a random act of violence? While Fran and I couldn't be certain, it seemed to me unlikely that someone seeking to commit a random crime of violence would drive along a gravel road in a country residential area, enter a three-tenths-mile-long driveway, go past a house at the fork in the driveway, go past a kennel of Saint Bernards, and enter a house where a Saint Bernard roamed loose to murder someone he or she didn't know, particularly since the victim wasn't raped or robbed. Every time we talked about the possibilities, Fran felt the odds of the killing being random were virtually nil. I agreed completely.

Another theory we had to consider was that Marlys might have been involved in something bad and someone had come to settle the issue with her. Would that person have been so anxious to hurt her that he or she struck first, before a verbal confrontation? What could Marlys have done to prompt someone to come to the house and attack her? The odds of this were also very slim, if not negligible, not only because of the way the assault happened. What could Marlys have done? She had a clean record repeatedly examined under the microscope of law enforcement looking to solve a murder. Most every mother thinks her child is beyond fault; investigators don't have that same parental bias. Each officer involved in this case had done his best to find some "dirt" about Marlys that might provide a motive they could follow to a potential murderer. They found nothing.

A more possible theory was that Marlys had a boyfriend or a suitor who became angry enough with her to commit murder. But none of her boyfriends over the three or four years leading up to the attack had any reason to harm her. The relationships were low key, not dramatic or highly emotional. She wasn't pregnant. She hadn't had a recent confrontation with anyone she dated. Of course they needed to be cleared, and investigators would verify that her former boyfriends went on to ordinary lives.

Fran knew with nearly absolute certainty that Marlys entered the house on the ground floor, came through the family room, walked past the stairs to the second level. Others who didn't know her routine would expect an eighteen-year-old girl to go upstairs first. The person who struck Marlys followed her into the small office just past the stairway, attacking her as she turned. Fran worried that Marlys might have surprised someone in the home. Patience had been locked up in the master bedroom on the second level. Knowing the dog and her habits as Fran did, she believed someone put her there, probably before the attack, before Marlys arrived home. Valuables lay in plain sight in Fran's bedroom. Cash sat on the desk in the office where Marlys's murderer struck her down, yet nothing had been taken.

For days Fran and I went over and over all the questions that were raised by the confession and Ture's recantation of it. Who else would even be in the house, let alone want to harm her daughter? Was Marlys even the intended victim? The confession said Ture had gone to the house to kill Fran. Wasn't it much more logical for Fran, rather than Marlys, to go to the little office? Wasn't it more likely that someone who wanted to harm Fran would have known about the house and its layout, known even when Fran was expected home in the afternoon? She had asked herself those questions practically from day one. She still had not overcome the thought that she had been punished because of her relationship with me. She had just begun to have a happy life and a hope for the future—or an affair, as some would call it—and her happiness might not have pleased others. Why did Ture's recanted confession refer to an argument between Fran and Greg, then quote Greg? Over and over, Fran asked these questions of the authorities, even in the face of the two alibis: Ture was at work and Greg was on the airplane.

Marlys was murdered by someone who had no legitimate reason for being in the house. Nothing Marlys did would justify her being annihilated. Yet she did something: she came home, entered her own house, walked in as if life were normal, and was struck down. Her innocence had been shattered by the monster wielding that heavy weapon.

By 1983 it became clear that I would have to move on in my career. We talked about a change in employment as if it were a cancer to be dealt with, clinically, objectively. Moving again was out of the question; even if we could have found the energy, we couldn't relocate our already once-displaced family. Having no real choice, we decided to stay in Philadelphia, and I would start my own law practice.

Fran used some of her divorce settlement money to take the two of us to Jamaica for a week on the beach. This vacation had been her dream, and it might be a long time before we had another chance.

Fran picked seashells all day long while I watched from behind my book. We were looking for answers, not mere survival. On the beach, watching a sunset, Fran took my hand and squeezed it. She said, "I want to be healed. If I can't have Marlys back, and I know I can't now, I want to be healed."

Healing is not an easy thing to come by, however, and much more than an intellectual decision is needed. Fran began having health problems, derived, we later learned, from her repressed grief. She felt trapped in a cage where she couldn't even say Marlys's name out loud without crying. She fought to keep her feelings in. I would ask "What's wrong?" and she couldn't reply. Back then, we didn't know how to talk out our problems and fears.

The symptoms got worse. Finally, Fran's doctor asked, "Has anything stressful happened to you recently?" The floodgates of tears opened, leading to several more visits, then to a recommendation for counseling, which in turn led to our pastor. This minister, divinely inspired, didn't try to give Fran answers. Instead, he suggested that she meet with a new group just forming in nearby Valley Forge, called The Compassionate Friends. Fran went, finding a self-help support group for people whose children have died. There it was all right to cry when speaking of a deceased child. No one tried to provide answers; everyone offered compassion. Fran heard others speak of the same fears and anguish she had experienced—even thoughts of suicide. Some resented the fact that their child was dead and someone else's "brat" still made mischief. Fran says, "The Compassionate Friends saved my life. Just understanding it is good to grieve has been that important in our lives."

Looking for understanding in another forum, I continued to read theology, talk to clergy, study what people wrote about God. I wanted answers. One Sunday we attended a service for all those in the congregation who had gone on to a religious calling. Some were in seminary, others were ordained. On the way home, I said to Fran, "Wouldn't it be funny if I went to seminary?" Two months later, Fran was on The Compassionate Friends board in Valley Forge and I was at seminary, studying theology.

The two paths, self-help and study, pointed at the same goal: to heal from the intense pain of bereavement and find a way to look toward the future. Dealing with grief so that it didn't destroy our lives required us first to recognize that we were grieving and second to adopt a new way of life. The "American way" doesn't recognize the needs of the bereaved, expecting men to be tough and women to cry a bit, then both to get back to ordinary activities. The safe-house concept of gathering as a group to share inner feelings doesn't fit with what the nonbereaved consider to be normal, and our contact with them decreased. Healing required a radical conversion from fixation on our own feelings to an acquired ability to see those same feelings in others, and to offer assurances that their reactions are just as normal for them as they had been for us.

In August 1985 we moved Marlys's casket from Minnesota to the cemetery near our home in Pennsylvania. We had put our roots there, we concluded. Fran felt relieved and happy to be able to tend the grave again. By then she could accept the reality of Marlys's death.

We were making progress on other matters as well. I began to help Fran facilitate meetings at The Compassionate Friends and helped her write presentations she made to bereaved parents. We were in transition again, as Fran began to allow me into her grief process as a stepparent. We began to understand that every individual—a bereaved mother, an older brother or younger sister, even a stepparent or stepchild—has pain. We learned that it isn't right to say "My pain is greater than yours." Our own pain is all we truly know. Picture two patients in the hospital, each with a different medical problem; each hurts. How can one compare the pain of cancer to that of a heart attack? Likewise, each person grieves differently, with intensely personal emotions.

After Marlys died, Fran bought a new piano, and it has been with us every place we've lived, sometimes out of tune but always available to play. I like to sit near, reading or thinking. Fran doesn't play for me, but lets me into her world. The piano is her mental health barometer: she plays often when her emotional wellness is rising, infrequently when life becomes heavy. There wasn't much music in our lives in the first decade without Marlys.

We found ourselves adrift, separated more and more from the life we had once expected to live. First Ray and then JD married in 1988. Lynn, her husband, and their three children moved back to Minnesota. Maria, her husband, and their son moved one county further away, and Shawn went off to college.

We were in full retreat now from the nonbereaved, emotionally running away from that part of our lives in Pennsylvania. We purchased a one-bedroom condominium in Ocean City, Maryland, as a weekend getaway. We began to look for other reasons to be away from where we had transplanted our roots. I moved part of my intellectual property law practice to Maryland. I began writing seriously, starting another steep learning curve.

Just over a year after we bought our condo, we closed on the sale of our house in Pennsylvania, left town, and became Maryland residents. We moved into a town house on the bay next to the condo. Fran bought a new convertible to use in Ocean City, and I leased a large sedan to commute to the significant part of my law practice remaining in Pennsylvania. I converted the condo to an office.

In Ocean City, we developed a routine: I would drive up to Pennsylvania for three or four days of work at a law firm, then drive back for a long weekend. When I came home, Fran always had a special meal prepared. After dinner, if the weather permitted, we would sit on the deck, talking. Of course the unsolved crime led the list of topics, and so did the desire to reach out to others. We began to see a need for a book to explain our understanding of where God is in all the pain and sorrow of tragedies.

I had notebooks full of reflections and a pretty good idea of how I wanted to structure the book, but both of us wanted it to have Fran's perspective. She was the mother. She "lost" a child to murder. She had the grief and pain. She had recently spoken to a nursing class at a community college in northern Virginia about the symptoms of grief. This seemed like a good way to start the work on the book, and I thought it would be useful as part of Fran's participation in the writing. I asked her to dictate the talk she had given. She said she didn't want to do it again—it would be too painful.

We argued for a day or so, and then I said, "If you want to be part of this book, get out on the deck. Take the tape recorder. Talk the talk you just gave."

"I can't," Fran said.

"Yes, you can," I said, then pointed to the chair on the deck. "All you have to do is talk. Give your lecture."

Fran went out on the deck and I went upstairs to my office. In her chair, Fran cried—sobbed. *It's so painful, and I don't want to deal with it. I made it through the lecture because I had people in front of me I could educate. I'm not helping anyone out here, talking to a stupid machine.* She felt absolutely alone, abandoned. Then she thought back to the first days after Marlys's funeral, when Gwen Peterson told her to do laundry, peel potatoes for supper, write thank-you notes. She began to dictate, feeling the intense pain of each word. When she finished, she came up to my office. "Here it is," she said, looking angry, her face still tear-stained. "I don't know how you'll use it, but I did it. You say it was something I had to do, but I didn't want to."

"Thanks. I really think it is important," I said.

"You are unreasonable. You know I didn't want to do it again, after that class. You don't know how hard it was. So I sat on the deck with a damnable tape recorder."

Something changed in Fran that day. She says now that the dictating session on the deck helped her finally realize she had to let me in to her grief. We worked on the book together after that. I would draft a section, Fran would read it out loud to me, we would talk about it, and the chapters grew. "People in that much pain don't read long chapters," she said, so we divided them in half. "There needs to be more space between sections in the chapters." We did that, and Fran's talent at design and laying out texts, developed over years of doing newsletters, helped make it an easier book to read. When she and I wrote the book and published it, she felt cleansed and needed. We were becoming partners on an even deeper level.

In February 1991 we published the first edition of *I Wasn't Ready,* written to explore the healing process and present theological reflections on life after Marlys's murder. An editor at Augsburg Fortress Press later would say, "The book pinpoints the weakness at the heart of Christian theology—its non-answer to evil—and moves around that weakness to facilitate what Christians *can* provide: accompaniment." He was right, of course; we don't have an answer for why evil exists, but we do offer comfort. If the pain we suffer from bereavement isn't the very definition of evil, no matter how the death occurs, I will never know what is. Intense grief can ruin lives. At best it is difficult to face. Grief is avoided when possible, rejected when it is not personal, and understood if at all only by a few.

Our pain in the loss of a loved one is as intense as physical torture. It comes from within us in our anguish because the one we loved is gone. Out of that tragedy, sustained by our love for the one who has died, encouraged by the love of others who comforted us, peace came. It took a long time to get there, but without love, I'm convinced, peace never would have arrived.

One Saturday night at the town house in Ocean City, the telephone rang after Fran had gone to bed. I went to the phone quickly, so it would not wake her, and I went with concern. Who expects good news when the phone rings late on Saturday night?

It was a collect call from a county jail, person to person for me. I didn't recognize the name but accepted the charges, then listened in fascination as the caller told me how his mother was in the hospital, overcome with grief with the death of her daughter. His sister had been murdered just a few days ago. His mother couldn't cope with her grief. He begged me to go to her, saying, "I hope you can help my mother survive."

I didn't wake Fran that night but went to bed with my anxiety. I found myself in the midst of an adventure I did not want. Fran and I found healing when we reached out to others, but why did we have to respond to a call from prison? As I went to sleep, I knew we had to go, but it wasn't a happy prospect.

The next morning I told Fran about the call. She remembered hearing about the murder on the local news and called the hospital to check on the mother's condition. After talking to several people on the floor, and finally talking to a supervisor, she found a nurse who happened to be the niece of a leader of the local Compassionate Friends chapter. She had heard about our book. The nurse said, "Yes, please come. I think you can give her hope."

When we entered the hospital room, we found a woman lying in bed, curled up on her side in a fetal position, tears streaming down her face, a picture of absolute despair. Fran told her that she too was the mother of a daughter who had been murdered.

Her eyes opened slightly and she said, "Then you understand."

Fran told her, "Your daughter wouldn't want you like this." Fran held on to the bed rail. "I don't have all the answers, but I want you to see I made it. You can, too."

The two mothers talked for about an hour. No one mentioned the surveillance camera above the bed and the other signs that the hospital was concerned about suicide. No one told her to be strong for her other children, although it was clear that they needed her. Fran told the woman she would someday be able to reach out to others, but in the meantime, others were there for her. Fran said, "Get out of the hospital. Surround yourself with people who care about you so you can grieve. I was a stranger until today, until your son cared about you and called us."

The woman asked Fran if it hurt for her to be there, and Fran responded, "Yes, but it makes my own daughter's death mean more."

The woman's mother, also at the hospital, seemed overwhelmed with trying to help her daughter survive in this tragic situation. She asked if Fran would be attending the funeral. Fran said both she and I would go if the mother of the murdered girl wanted us to be there. "Do you want me to come to the funeral?" Fran asked.

The woman no longer lay curled up on her side. She said, "Yes, if it doesn't hurt too much, I want you to come to the funeral." She had taken her first step. Healing begins, even in the deepest grief, when a person feels concern for others.

Fran and I did something else that day, something that took much more courage. We went to the prison to visit the son who had asked us to help his mother. As we drove, we talked about going to a place that locks up people who commit crimes like murder, where people like the one who killed Marlys should be. "We're going," Fran said, "because the young man cared enough about his mother to call us." In a way, we also went out of curiosity. Could we ever visit someone in prison? Did we have within us the concept of compassion for someone who had done evil?

The next day, we went to the funeral. Afterward, Fran kept in contact with the mother, encouraging her. During one telephone call some months later, this grieving mother told Fran, "You were there at the right time for me. No matter how bad I feel, no matter how much I cry, and I still do a lot of both, I always remember that you came to see me, you let me see hope, you saved me from despair. And I thank God for you. I thank a God who didn't exist for me in any real way until you came along. Thank you."

Sometimes people ask, "Is there life after tragedy?" Yes, Fran and I say, life does go on, painfully, even agonizingly for a while, defined and sustained by memories. We survived tragedy and achieved what healing we may have in our love for each other, for Marlys and our other children, for others who are hurting, for anyone beyond ourselves. Fran responded to the woman in the hospital out of love, which also gave us the courage to go to the prison.

Part III

Reviving the Investigation

11

Seeking Justice Now

"*I* MADE A CALL," Fran said, "to the Washington County sheriff's office this morning." We were having breakfast coffee on the deck in Ocean City. "Wasted a call, I should say. I asked what they had done lately, and he just talked about not having time to work on leads."

"You'd think they'd find the time," I answered, stating the obvious, "after fourteen years." We had settled into the town house, continued the life of exile. We were facing southwest, watching the water as birds circled and boats made their way to and from. The slosh of the waves and the tide on the piers mingled with the sound of our conversation.

"I trusted the system," she said, "and it let me down. It's 1993 and the killer is still free, able to enjoy life, while Marlys can't, didn't have a chance to live. She had the whole world waiting for her. She was just eighteen, Jack."

"We need to do something," I said after a moment. "Marlys and the murder are always on my mind, too." Fran's eyes began to tear, the sadness once again opening the wound that never seemed to heal. "Last night," I went on to say, "I had some heavy dreams. The first started as a nice scene at a lovely place, with you and the kids. Then a cop showed up. He seemed nice until he separated me from you and the others. Then he at-tacked me, laughing. He had an ugly dog with a hand grenade in its mouth."

"That's ridiculous. What happened?"

"I started to wake up, and then I took over the dream. I told him I'd mash him and his dog into paste. I called the feds, and completely woke up. When I went back to sleep, I dreamed about being lost, wandering, being kept from others, only hearing a cry in my head—'Help me, Daddy'—over and over, a daughter crying."

"Marlys?" Fran asked, hoping I would tell her something about her daughter, even from a dream.

"Who else? The demons inside me were trying to get out, and I couldn't do a thing about it."

"I'm at my wits' end about what to do."

"Me, too. Maybe." I felt the silence building between us as we stared out at the water, as if there were answers floating amid the waves. "One thing," I said, "my promise to Marlys was to take care of you, not to play detective. I've never tried to solve the crime. We had other children to raise. We needed to get on with life." Even as I said those words, I knew the emptiness of ever "getting on" without Marlys. Fran turned away. "But," I went on, "our responsibilities to the other children have eased. Maybe," I said, more as a question, "we could work together to solve the crime? Maybe my dreams are telling us we should?"

"Why would we do better than the cops?"

"We can't do worse."

"Do we hire a private detective?" she asked, gathering energy as she spoke.

"I don't think so. First thing we can try is to push the investigators. Let's find out what they've really been doing all these years. Expose them. Let the world see what little has been done. If you want to, that is." At least we were looking at each other again. "Are you sure you're ready?"

"I will do anything," Fran said, then pointed to a butterfly passing by the railing to the deck. As she spoke, first this one, then several, and soon dozens, maybe hundreds of the graceful creatures appeared from around the corner of our building, coursing south over the bay. We were surrounded by floating, darting orange and black monarchs, symbols of new life. Our exile had ended. We had made a simple decision. From that moment on, working to solve the crime would be as natural as a butterfly's migration.

We often talked about the investigation while we watched one of the two television shows Fran insisted on viewing— *America's Most Wanted* and *Unsolved Mysteries*. These programs had become part of her effort to keep the investigation alive, to find a way to solve the murder. She hoped that somehow a new procedure would show up to help solve the case. So often, she had seen crimes being solved when the perpetrator was identified and others came forward with new evidence. Her dream was to be able to do the same thing.

One night we had a special interest in *Unsolved Mysteries*. I had seen the previews and recognized Professor James E. Starrs, a forensic expert featured on that night's program. "I know that guy," I told Fran. "I had him as a professor in law school back in the 1960s."

Professor Starrs now taught law at George Washington University Law School in Washington, D.C. He also taught forensic science as a member of that university's School of Arts and Sciences, and had a national reputation as a forensic expert. Starrs talked about trying to identify the body of John Wilkes Booth. "Call him," Fran demanded. "If he's that good, ask him to look at our case."

Agreeing that Starrs might be able to help, I wrote a letter to my former professor instead of calling. I wanted to phrase my appeal in a way that would be as compelling as the need Fran had to ask him to help. While I worked on the letter, Fran called the investigator in the Washington County sheriff's office, Deputy Dale Fuerstenberg, telling him what we planned. He didn't object, and even said that the sheriff's office would cooperate with anyone who was working for her.

I showed Fran the draft. This is the main text as I sent it:

I am a former student of yours, taking several of your courses in the 1960s at DePaul College of Law, where I graduated in 1967. I have good memories of those courses. I was also excited to recognize you on the *Unsolved Mysteries* television show and pleased that you have achieved an impressive reputation in forensic sciences.

I would like to believe I would write to offer my congratulations and to say that I remember you well even if that were my only reason for writing. But my reason is more important than that. Enclosed is a copy of a book I wrote and published that looks at the healing process that my wife experienced after the murder of her daughter in 1979. *I Wasn't Ready* deals with issues of healing grief and has a theological perspective. Healing is important.

We have come to understand that another aspect of grief, forgiveness, is also important, particularly if one seeks to fully return to normal living. While it may be true that we will only understand evil when we face God, from a theological perspective, it is also true that seeking justice in this world is something that brings understanding now. . . .

All this means that I would like to make an appointment to visit with you to renew our acquaintance and to talk with you . . . about helping us with Marlys's murder. The sheriff in charge of the investigations is looking forward to your potential help. . . . It is my hope that something good can come from that conversation.

"I like what you said about seeking justice," Fran said, handing the letter back. "This isn't theological with me, but I like that part, too. There is too much missing in my life besides Marlys herself. Maybe justice is the piece I need to be whole again."

Professor Starrs called in response to the letter and expressed willingness to see what he could do, if not to solve the crime then at least to explore the issues. Based on what we told him, and as part of his larger circle of contacts, he called a long-term friend at the Minnesota Bureau of Criminal Apprehension (BCA). He also spoke with Dale Fuerstenberg. Starrs asked Fran for her files, including reports, photographs, factual information. He wanted X-rays, toxicological data, diagrams, and photographs, as well as copies of all the newspaper articles.

Initially we were excited, learning about technological advances such as getting fingerprints from clothing. We wracked our brains for anything that would have been in contact with the killer, with no luck. Starrs wanted photographs of fingerprints that were found, blood spatter patterns. He told us that if he got into the case, "it [would] be up to my hip boots, but I have to have access to all the evidence." I wrote a power of attorney for him to act on Fran's behalf.

A while later I learned that Starrs had been to North Carolina, where he met Special Agent Everett Doolittle from Minnesota's BCA. Soon after Starrs came back to Washington, I took Fran to meet with him, spending two intense hours in a conference room at his law school. Starrs told us of his initial reaction: "It's possible," he said, "a stranger came in the house and killed Marlys in a panic. The deliberateness of the attack leads me to conclude that the killer felt outraged for being repulsed over something said, or for having been rejected."

Fran listened in wonder. No one in Minnesota had ever suggested this to her. She or Marlys knew every suspect they asked her about. Her mind raced back to the confession—by a stranger, no less. Could there be truth in those pages? Had we overlooked something? Then she remembered his alibi. It couldn't be him.

Starrs painted a bleak picture of the work done to date. No diagrams or photographs of Marlys had been made or taken at the scene. The pathological autopsy determined the cause of death and other conditions of Marlys's body but didn't address forensic issues. A vaginal swab had been taken and analyzed but no report could be found. The murder weapon was a blunt instrument, not clearly identified. He had learned that some skull bone fragments were being kept by the BCA crime lab, but no cast had been made.

Doolittle led a BCA cold case unit. "He admitted his investigation remained in its infancy," Starrs said. "He's working full time on twelve different cases. How could anything get done?" Doolittle acknowledged that the crime could be solved only with pressure, from Starrs and others, to get a commitment for the manpower he needed for the investigative work still to be done. Doolittle had told Starrs that the case wouldn't get solved if outsiders left the investigators alone.

Trembling in anger, Fran said, "If pressure will help, we're only just beginning."

Fran began making even more calls to Washington County, asking about this cold case unit. "I'm involved now," she said often. She wanted to talk to Doolittle, but Fuerstenberg asked her to let the county handle it. "It will only confuse things," he said. The sheriff, Jim Trudeau, wanted his office to maintain control over the case.

Because we needed to be together full time as part of our new efforts, we moved back to Pennsylvania, back near Marlys's grave, and set up a base of operation. Spring arrived late in 1994. One storm after another wore us down. Ice formed on the eaves of the house, causing the roof to leak. Branches broke and one beautiful tree in the front yard split open, fatally damaged. Finally we decided we needed to escape and made plans to take a vacation. We decided on Padre Island, Texas.

It didn't dawn on me at first, but Fran wanted to go to this place for more than sun and sea. We walked the beach, disappointed with tar pollution and a lack of seashells to collect. We went to the places that Fran remembered Marlys, Ray, and Lynn talking about when their father took them to Padre during summer visits. We tried to get a sense of what it had been like for Marlys, especially since we could no longer ask her. Lynn and Ray sometimes talked about having fun, but was there something special about this island?

We rented a convertible like the one we had at home and drove around the small island. "Go that way," Fran pointed, "and I'll show you the hotel where I was when Ray had his accident."

"Where you were on the phone with me?"

"Yes." A few minutes later we saw the hotel, now under a different name. "Over there is where I got my suntan and Lynn met some boys she talked to."

At dinner that night at that hotel, I said, "I think the cops need to talk to that guy who worked for Greg at the body shop. I still remember how he tried to ignore us when he saw us together at the lumberyard a few months after the funeral."

"I remember," Fran said. "He moved to Florida so quickly after that. Maybe he knew what his son supposedly knew."

On the deck of the rented condo, Fran brought up Lynn's ex-boyfriend. "I wonder if he was on drugs and Marlys surprised him when she came home?"

"He dropped Lynn so quickly," I said. "Maybe his conscience bothered him."

"Whoever it was, if they were on drugs they might not even remember killing her."

We imagined a scenario during a walk on the beach the next day. Fran would soon be going to Minnesota for a meeting investigators had set up with KSTP, a local television station. Fran would be part of a television spot to bring publicity to the crime.

We imagined a script. Fran would be asked, "Was there something unusual at the time of the murder?"

She would reply, "On Sunday night Marlys acted strangely, but we didn't really suspect anything."

"How," the reporter would ask, "was she acting strange?"

Then Fran would say, "Marlys came home, not her bubbly

self, just sitting in front of the living room window, looking out, staring, absorbed in something we never learned."

"What could it have been?" he would ask.

Not being sarcastic, but wistful, she would say, "We'd know a lot, wouldn't we, if we learned what was bothering her."

"Any theories?" he would ask.

"Lots," she would say. "Like maybe Marlys saw some guys doing or selling drugs, or she might have seen boys fooling around. Maybe someone threatened her because she wouldn't date him." Marlys had been threatened, we did know, by a guy on a motorcycle the Friday before her death. Fran might mention that, but what she most certainly wanted to say was, "Someone knows something. If you're out there today, please . . ."

We didn't know what the guy had said to Marlys, but we knew it had caused a scene and the manager made him leave. For years we had asked, pressured, pleaded with the investigators to talk to the owners and employees of the café.

Later, Fran spoke about needing to come to Padre Island. "I don't know why," she said. "Maybe I'm dumb, but now I don't have to come here again. Being here makes me think of when Marlys's friends helped pack up her room. It was such a sad and sorrowful thing to imagine going through the shortened lifetime accumulations of a young woman. Jack, she even had seashells from Padre Island, each wrapped in tissue by her friends so they wouldn't break. I found them recently as I was going through things.

"She would be thirty-three now, if she were alive. Her father rented a motor home and they came down here from Houston. Marlys was such a little girl, so bright and sparkling like the sea, so innocent, collecting seashells. Just today on the beach, I watched a child's sand castle being washed away by the waves rolling in. One wave and it's gone. A life should not be like that. If I can't have Marlys back, I want justice. I want the one who struck her down to face me, to tell me why the blows were struck. Someone knows why! We won't rest until we have justice."

After we returned to Pennsylvania, Dale Fuerstenberg called to tell Fran about a newspaper article concerning the murder. The headline "Investigative Team Moves in to Crack Wohlenhaus Murder" covered the width of the front page of the *St. Croix Valley Press.* A picture of Marlys, looking back over her shoulder, had been positioned by the headline, as if she were watching the efforts of those seeking to solve the crime. The article announced formation of an investigative team from Washington County and the Minnesota Bureau of Criminal Apprehension cold case unit and told of a telephone call to the sheriff's department in which a local resident gave some "details" about the victim. The article confirmed Fuerstenberg's longtime dedication but also acknowledged that his work, all on his own time and not part of the department's efforts, was the only work being done on the case until the formation of this new unit.

Fuerstenberg told Fran the article had sparked local activity; more calls were coming in. He said there were leads now, and once again the case would be actively investigated. For the first time in more than ten years, law enforcement officials offered hope that the crime might be solved.

Fran asked Fuerstenberg, "What do we have to do?"

"Nothing yet," he replied, "but someone from the BCA will be getting in touch with you soon."

Although the excitement gave us encouragement, both Fran and I felt overwhelmed. And very angry. As we sat in the living room, looking at each other and thinking of the years we had waited for this effort, an overpowering need for justice and for answers burst forth like a monsoon flood. In a moment of panic, I asked Fran, "How come I never imagine myself trying to investigate the case? I never fantasize me being one who solves crimes, like fictional detectives. I still don't picture myself solving the crime, but I see myself carrying out judgment, and that makes me afraid."

"I can't get angry," she said, "until I know who to be angry with. But I am upset. Nothing has been done for so many years."

"I think our talking with Professor Starrs has helped move this along. It's the pressure we're applying as much as anything else."

Fran received another phone call, this time from Special Agent Doolittle, who said the BCA cold case unit was looking at Marlys's murder and asked if he could come to Pennsylvania to talk about the case.

Was there ever an easier question to answer?

12

Beginning to Participate

*F*RAN FELT LIKE SHE WAS WAITING FOR SANTA CLAUS, full of expectations, anticipating the arrival of Special Agent Everett Doolittle from Minnesota. When he introduced himself, he laughingly stroked his short gray beard and pointed to his receding hairline, saying, "I wear this because I'm losing the hair on top." The three of us settled into the breakfast room, at the large gray table where Doolittle could spread out his files, make notes, "do my thing," as he said. "All I do is work on cold cases, ones that weren't solved initially and ended up on a shelf."

"Our case sure did," Fran said.

"I know," Doolittle replied, "and now I'm working on it. But in most of them I know who committed the crime." His words were precise, not quite clipped, and he spoke with a friendly Minnesota accent. He told us how he organized the case file, adding that he didn't see a very high solvability factor, as he called it, because there were no witnesses and no weapon had been found.

Both Fran and I were shocked, even angry, to learn that so many things had not been done. No nationwide computer check for similar crimes had been made. Incredibly, Doolittle had just recently begun creating the first time line—fifteen years after the murder.

The highest probability, he told us, was that Marlys knew the killer and had some connection with him. The main problem preventing a successful effort would be if we didn't get enough support and interest from the county attorney's office. "Without the county's active participation," he said, "we aren't going to solve the crime. Even with their support," he added, "it's no sure thing at all."

Turning on his tape recorder, he began the formal interview: "This is Special Agent Everett Doolittle with the Minnesota Bureau of Criminal Apprehension, this is BCA Case 90000198. This is an interview being conducted with Fran, ah, Fran, can I have your full name and date of birth?"

Fran replied, and a few more questions established the time and place of the interview. He started from the beginning. He took notes in addition to the taping while Fran once again told her story of coming home to find Marlys. She tried to remember everything, each detail, exhausted all the memory she had.

When she finished, Doolittle turned off the recorder. "Jack," he said, "I'm not going to take another statement from you. Fran told me where you were, what you know, and that's been verified several times."

"So I'm not a suspect?" I asked, wondering if it mattered to have this fact on the record.

"Well, one guy thinks you are, but we won't go into that."

The three of us then began going over each possible suspect. Rather than focus on a person because he might be guilty, Doolittle said, he intended to clear each individual. "In time, there should only be one guy left, and if we can't clear him, we'll have found the one who killed Marlys."

We talked first about Tom Cartony, who lived across the back hill behind the house on Trading Post Trail and who had been Deputy Sheriff Dale Fuerstenberg's favorite suspect. According to friends of Marlys, Cartony wanted to date her, but she had called him a "scumbag" and word got around that he said he was going to harm her. Doolittle had talked with him; Cartony was married and had at least one child. "This means he doesn't have a history of such things, and while that doesn't clear him, I don't have him at the top of the list," Doolittle said. "And I am going to go with him out of state to verify his alibi."

Dennis Sipe, a drifter who lived in the woods, had called in a tip about Tom Cartony. Sipe had a reputation, unproved, for violence against women. Lynn's boyfriend lived up the gully and over the hill from the house. Several students had said he left school early on the day of the murder. Two days after the murder, he told Lynn he didn't want to see her again, and shortly after that his parents checked him in to a medical program. Scott Swanson, an ex-boyfriend of Marlys, had threatened her. He also hung around with Jim Fibeson, who had a car that looked like the one seen leaving the property.

Later we talked about Greg Loux again. He was still in the air at the time of the murder. He bought a stranger a drink, took his business card, and when his plane arrived he took so long to come from the gate to where Ray was picking him up that Ray called the body shop to double-check whether Greg had made the flight. Doolittle had interviewed him at least once and said he was convinced Greg had nothing to do with Marlys's death. "He's felt the grief, too," Doolittle said. "But you're right, we have to clear him like everyone else."

Shortly after the murder, someone—we couldn't remember who—said that one of the sons of the foreman at Greg's Body Shop knew who killed Marlys but didn't reveal a name. Was that why the father moved away? Doolittle said he would check it out.

For some reason, we didn't talk about Joe Ture, other than to say that his alibi may have cleared him but the confession would make it difficult to convict anyone else. We talked all day Saturday, finally taking a break for dinner out, away from the house, if not from the tension. We both felt enormous stress, being dragged through the ugly, violent memories.

Doolittle left on Sunday morning, after twenty exhaustive and exhausting hours of dialogue. I perceived him to be a man doing what he loves to do. Fran said he just might be her Columbo. That morning we went to church, drained to empty. Fran cried quietly during the service, saying that the pain had come back almost as intensely as in the beginning. She recovered during the long afternoon we spent rehashing the information we now had about the crime. "We can be beyond the pain," she said that evening, "but never beyond the loss. Pain is ongoing, but there's life beyond it. I miss Marlys and I always will, but I'm beyond the totally incapacitating pain."

"Except on days like today," I replied.

"I know all about today," she said, "but I want people to know there is hope and there is life after tragedy if we work at it. We'll learn from this, maybe help others."

Two weeks later, Fran found herself strapped into a lie detector unit. Doolittle had called to say that he wanted her to take the test because he was having problems with some of the suspects who had initially refused to cooperate. "If you take one, then how can they decline?" he had asked. During the test, Fran became curious about the questions. They seemed to spend a lot of time on her relationship with me, not prying on details of the past but focusing on the present. She was honest, having nothing to hide.

When spring came, we flew to Minnesota for a meeting and Fran's first appeal to the public for help. We met Doolittle at the Bureau of Criminal Apprehension. After passing through security, we waited in his second-floor office as we watched a television crew set up. Doolittle sat at his desk against the far wall; behind him the staff had filled a large blackboard with information on the dozen or so cases on his docket, showing important dates, status, and names. Some items were covered up for this meeting to protect the privacy of the victims and possible perpetrators. Fran shuddered at seeing people's names and important dates so familiar to her listed on a board next to other unsolved crimes. "Solidarity," she whispered to me, pointing to the list. Victims everywhere had become part of her life.

After Doolittle and a Washington County deputy were interviewed, Fran told her story, talking directly into the camera, script in mind, wondering if someone would hear her plea to come forward. During the taping, KSTP-TV commentator Tom Hauser did his best to be kind, not really knowing what to say to the mother of a murdered young woman.

KSTP ran the two-minute news feature of Fran and the law enforcement officers on Mother's Day, May 8, timed to air on the fifteenth anniversary of the attack on Marlys. Later we were told that the broadcast brought some responses, but nothing concrete.

Fran returned to Minnesota one more time in 1994 to present a workshop at a Parents of Murdered Children national conference. Before the conference, Fran met with Washington County Attorney Dick Arney and Assistant County Attorney Rick Hodsdon at the courthouse. When she told her story, apologized for crying, and pleaded with them, Hodsdon allowed himself to have feelings for the case. Normally, he took precautions before committing himself to a courageous effort; in court he wore a bulletproof vest because he specialized in prosecuting gangs and drug cases. That day he absorbed the full impact of Fran's story.

After the meeting, he told Arney that he wanted the case. "I'll take it even if the sheriff drops the investigation," he said. When he was asked why, Hodson drummed his fingers on the table. "This happened in our county. I need to make it right."

Lynn joined Fran at the conference meetings that afternoon and stayed at the hotel with her. They finally found a way to deal with the individual and separate grief each suffered, one losing a daughter and the other a sister. Lynn felt proud of her mom and her poise speaking to the group, saw her shining as she helped others with their pain.

During a break, Fran and Lynn found a quiet alcove at the hotel. "When we read The Compassionate Friends credo at our meetings," Fran said, "we also read the one for siblings."

"I've never gone to a meeting," Lynn replied.

"I know. It's up to the individual, and I'm not pushing it at all. I just wanted to say that the credo describes siblings as the forgotten mourners. I haven't helped you much."

"Yes, you have," Lynn said. "Maybe we haven't talked about it much, but I see what you do for others. I read the newsletter you do every month."

"That's not much," Fran said, tears forming.

"I wasn't easy to talk to," Lynn said, "back then."

"Who was? But I want you to know how proud of you I am. And I want to say that I never tried to have you take Marlys's place. You are special, and you are you. The credo also says 'we aren't our sister or brother' as an affirmation of you being a survivor."

"I think I know the difference between replacing Marlys and remembering her. I'm going to nursing school because of her. Remember when my teddy bear got chewed up by one of the dogs, and Marlys sewed it back together? I wish I'd saved the note where she wrote 'Cured by Doctor Marlys.'"

Doolittle joined Fran and Lynn for lunch. He asked Fran to revisit the Joe Ture confession. Doolittle was going to interview Ture at the prison where he was serving a life sentence for the murder of Diane Edwards; the circumstances were in some ways like the attack on Marlys. "We have to clear him," Doolittle said, "because his confession is grounds for reasonable doubt in any trial of anyone else charged with the murder."

Back home, Fran went over Ture's confession point by point and wrote Doolittle a letter with our comments. But he was busy on another case.

In the spring of 1995 I formed my own law firm. The new arrangement gave me more control over how I spent my time.

In part, this change led to a new approach in solving Marlys's murder. We knew we had to be creative to keep the pressure on, to motivate law enforcement officers to work on our case rather than one of the other dozen also-deserving cases. We decided to use research for a new book as the vehicle to stir up the community, even push people to come up with answers. Fran started the project, writing letters to friends and family announcing her efforts to collect memories of and stories about Marlys; she included an opportunity for each one to speculate on the murder investigation. We also announced our intention to go to Minnesota in June to meet with as many people as we could.

Our business in Minnesota began as we descended a long hill to the St. Croix River, which flows between Wisconsin and Minnesota. We were entering the valley of hope. I drove across the bridge into Minnesota, then south along the river to Afton and turned up the hill to Memorial Lutheran Church. Although we had moved Marlys's casket to Pennsylvania nearly ten years before, Fran had kept the original headstone as a place where Marlys's friends could drop by to say a prayer or share a thought. After our own quiet moments, we went to the church, now rebuilt as an addition to the old fellowship hall, to see the plaque on the large handmade wooden cross standing by the entrance, a gift in Marlys's memory.

We had lunch at Selma's Ice Cream Parlor in downtown Afton. Across from the park, Selma's had been a place for each of Fran's children to meet with their friends. Lynn and her friends had been hanging out at Selma's when Marlys drove by on the evening before the murder. Because Lynn spent the night with a girlfriend, that was the last time she saw Marlys.

When Fran talked with the owner, Laine McGee, we learned how little was being said about the case in the valley anymore. There was almost no publicity. Laine had never seen the reward poster, then for $20,000. During the conversation, Fran heard, for the first of many times, the outrage at the prying questions the investigators asked as they sought to find something bad Marlys had done. That they found nothing both comforted her and drove her to keep on with the quest. Before we left, Laine gave Fran the names of contacts at several local newspapers who might be willing to tell the story again. Although Laine was kind to Fran, her memory about those events so many years ago had become truly dim.

In our visits, we came up with some precious memories of Marlys. Dorothy Jedrzejek, whom Fran knew from the Girl Scouts years, invited us to her retirement home. Sweat and tears ran down her face as "Mrs. Jed" thought about Marlys. "It's so hard to remember just one thing. No matter what you asked her to do, she would do it. She might not like it but she'd do it, saying, 'It'll only be for a little while.' My consolation," Mrs. Jed added, "is that she's fine now and in heaven with my son Walter. When Walter was killed in a rock-climbing accident, I could understand, sort of, how an accident could happen. I had answers. Then when you called me and said a psychic had told you Marlys and Walter were happy, I felt so much better. Your call has been a comfort. I guess my consolation is that they're together."

Later we met with newly elected Washington County Sheriff Jim Frank. Fran told him she appreciated his continued attention to the case, allowing the state BCA to work on it as a cold case. Frank mentioned that the publicity we received was fortunate; one of the candidates who had run against him and worked on the case with the BCA could have pursued the case for his own publicity.

Politely but clearly, I said I hoped Frank wouldn't drop the case for the same reason. The sheriff didn't take my remark as a well-intended comment, and I got us off to a bad start with him. Both Frank's indignation and my concern were justified, however, and after talking a while more, we saw each other's side and made peace. We also learned that Captain Mike Johnson would be head of the investigation unit handling Marlys's case.

Johnson knew Fran and her children at the time of the murder. Sheriff Frank told us that Johnson, also a bereaved parent, had requested this assignment. He formed a team including a new officer, Jeff Klarich, and the original investigator, Jim Richter. Agent Doolittle of the BCA would be helping them.

The sheriff reluctantly admitted that the case might have been mishandled, not wanting to cast blame on the department he now led. "Washington County," he said, "back in 1979 didn't have the expertise to handle murder cases. None of the leadership knew what to do because there had been so few murders in the county." Sheriff Frank had come from the St. Paul police department, where big-city crime gave him the know-how the county needed. Frank said the team would be learning how to solve crimes, using ours as a case method of study. We spent an hour with the sheriff and concluded with polite words. After our meeting with the sheriff, we went to downtown Stillwater, where we called on two newspapers, telling the reporters how Sheriff Frank had promised to keep working on the case. Several news stories made mention of his commitment.

That evening we met with Denise Eisinger, one of Marlys's closest friends, at the baseball park at Afton-Lakeland school, where Fran's kids attended and where Fran worked as the school nurse after we were first married. Denise's older son was playing in a ball game. The conversation was so intense that Denise forgot to watch her son's turn at bat. We talked about what could have been learned early in the investigation. Denise knew about the two motorcycle incidents involving Marlys, on the Friday and Sunday before the attack, but she could add nothing specific. She gave us the names of people who worked at the café who might remember seeing the person who hassled Marlys. We felt sad that the cops had not done this part of the investigation, and angry because we had asked them so many times.

Sending Denise back to watch her son play, we left before the game ended to meet another of Marlys's best friends, Beth

Campbell, at the home of her mother, Elaine. Elaine had helped Fran pack her things when she moved out of the house. She had seen money on the desk—more than one hundred dollars—when she cleaned the office where Marlys was attacked. She was the only one to go into the room. Elaine said she wondered why the police didn't look for hair or dirt or some clue from the murderer. Fran didn't really know what had been done by the investigators at the scene, other than to take photographs of the room after Marlys had been taken to the hospital.

We talked about how Beth didn't go to see Marlys at the hospital. The day of the attack, many of Marlys's friends gathered at Beth's house. "I was there," Elaine said, "and didn't know how to help except to let them talk. They would laugh and remember a nice moment, then get very sad again."

"Do you remember the prayer?" Fran asked.

"That's right," Beth said. "We were sitting in a circle, and someone said a prayer. Then we went around the room and everybody said something, like a prayer or a wish."

Fran reached over to Beth, holding her hand. "Lynn has told us about that time," Fran said, tears falling again. "Don't mind me," she said. "I've been crying with everybody, but I really need to talk with you and everyone we've seen. You've been so kind."

To our surprise, we learned from Beth that photographs of Marlys had been projected at the cap and gown ceremony at graduation while a song by the group Earth, Wind and Fire played. Beth remembered a photo of Marlys eating a pot pie. Some of the friends tried to get the school to leave her chair empty at the ceremony but didn't win that one. Fran understood the classmates' need to remember, in contrast with the school's view that life goes on.

The next evening we met Becky Kirkpatrick across the river in Hudson, Wisconsin, to talk and to encourage her in her efforts to put pressure on law enforcement agencies working on the case. Becky, Denise, and Beth were special friends of Marlys whose lives have forever been changed, and who have never abandoned their friend to the past. Becky had done the most to keep personal contact with the investigators, almost making it a crusade. On a first-name basis with Everett Doolittle and the county cops, she called, and called back if they didn't return her call.

"Don't worry," Becky said. "I'll keep on bugging the sheriff and anyone else I can. You know, I think someone had come into the house looking for something. When Marlys came home at the wrong time, he attacked her to keep her from identifying him." It was a simple theory that turned on the possibility of Marlys being at the wrong place at the wrong time. Someone panicked, so she died. But none of us really knew.

13

48 Hours, *Finally*

*O*UR LIST OF QUESTIONS had grown considerably by the time we met with Special Agent Doolittle during that week of travels in the valley. "Who haven't you cleared?" I asked. "Who have you cleared?" Fran asked, knowing the list would be shorter.

Doolittle briefly went through a list of ten suspects, with details on those he still had questions about. Jerry LaPlante, the boy Marlys had been dating, had given a bad interview, so Doolittle wanted to talk to him again. Tom Cartony's story about being in another state didn't completely check out. Former boyfriend Jeff Sullivan's statement that he was in Missouri at the time had been proven true. An anonymous caller, who claimed to be afraid, suggested that the killer might be another young man, Dennis Sipe, whom no one seemed able to find.

These people were facing an official inquiry into their lives. Until they were cleared, all were suspects who had rights but who also might have taken a human life. Society set the guidelines for this kind of investigation, and, within those rules, if there might be an inconvenience for someone, neither Fran nor I was going to be concerned. Sure, at least nine suspects were innocent, maybe even the tenth. If the investigators could eliminate most of those suspects, Doolittle might get closer to knowing who killed Marlys. If he eliminated all of them, that would be a problem, but one we would rather have than suspecting so many people.

Doolittle told us he had talked with Scott Johnson, who had been found asleep in his car not far from Fran's house on the day of the murder. "He said he has had real problems over the years because he keeps hearing Marlys screaming." Did he go in the house to look for something and, in his fear or panic, kill Marlys because she surprised him? Did he kill her, then go out to his car, take drugs perhaps to calm down, then fall asleep? Doolittle couldn't say.

Conflicting aspects of the case swirled in Fran's head as she listened to Doolittle. *He really doesn't know what happened,* she thought. *Am I better off not knowing?*

"Did Marlys even have a chance to scream?" I asked. "The first blow had to have been so powerful."

"I don't know," he replied. Fran didn't like the answer, and said so. "What I do know," Doolittle said, "is that they found this guy asleep, and he has a history of drugs. I think, but I don't know for sure, that he's imagined it all." Doolittle returned the focus to Joe Ture, saying, "If I could tie him to Afton, I would charge him and get an indictment."

This information, so casually spoken, startled me. "All you need is someone seeing him there and you charge him?" I asked. "How about the owners of Gene Daniels Restaurant?"

"We're checking that," Doolittle said.

The written confession included a conversation Ture claimed he had with Marlys at the house. Fran and I had been stumped trying to figure how Marlys could have done anything else except walk into the house, go directly to the office, put the mail down, turn around, drop her purse and books as she was attacked, fall down, and lie there until Fran came. This had been the only scene to make any sense to either of us. What didn't occur to us then but what we began to see might have happened was a conversation taking place several days earlier, perhaps during the confrontation at the café. Did Ture ask for a date, somewhat like the confession states? If she turned him down, told him to leave, called him a name, would he have stalked her? We left Doolittle with nothing but questions.

Later that afternoon we drove back toward Afton. The sky to the south began to darken, then blacken, as a storm approached. I turned to Fran. "This is the time, in the movies, when the hero says, 'Looks like it's going to get rough,' and the heroine says, 'In more ways than one.'"

Fran looked at the clouds. "Those are the kind that spawn tornadoes."

We drove up to Trading Post Trail, heading toward Fran's old house. Almost as soon as we turned onto the gravel road, my radar detector started squawking. After a moment a sheriff's patrol car came over the rise. I was driving slowly and the two cars passed like ships in the night. Where were they in 1979?

At 30th Street, we stopped, trying to determine if someone could hear screams from the house if he sat in his car. No way. We drove up the driveway, one-tenth of a mile to the neighbor's house, then another tenth to the pole barn and the path that led to Paul Hunt's house. We stopped still one-tenth of a mile short of the house, now remodeled and owned by a stranger. He could have heard those screams only if he had been in the house. If she screamed.

I turned the car around, intending to leave the area by going the other way. The rain started, then increased in intensity, dark clouds making midafternoon into near night. Rain obscured my vision, wind buffeted the car. A downed tree blocked the road. I quickly turned around and drove toward the house again, not pausing as we raced past the driveway. I went onto 30th Street, glad to be away from tree-shrouded Trading Post Trail. For a long time the rain didn't abate, but finally we were able to outpace the storm. Driving fast now, I asked Fran, "What omen do you take from this?"

"Compare the power of the storm," Fran said, "with the intensity of our search for the murderer. We were kept from going the other way, and we had to go back to where the suspect was in his car. That could be the connection we need to solve this case."

I wasn't so sure. "Maybe," I said, "the storm is more an acknowledgment that our search has just begun to get rough."

On the way home to Pennsylvania, Fran asked me what we had accomplished on the trip. The new sheriff wasn't happy with us, but the publicity the visit generated and the few news articles would keep the case before the residents of the St. Croix Valley. Dale Fuerstenberg had told Fran that if she went home and didn't call, didn't keep the pressure on, nothing would be done and the case wouldn't be solved. If she wanted closure and justice, instead of mere peace without justice, she would have to be a pain in the ass to everyone involved.

A strange thing had happened in Minnesota while we were looking for memories of Marlys. Both of us were doing research, trying to find the story we wanted to tell. I started the trip telling Fran I saw our lives as a love story interrupted by a tragedy. Fran said she wanted to find a way to be with Marlys again. On the way home, I became the one looking for memories, wanting those times so familiar to Fran. She didn't need her imagination in order to make her time with Marlys real. We had different goals now, Fran looking to solve the crime and me wanting to share the past.

I felt like we were living in two nearly parallel universes. One world, secret and within us all the time, focused on Marlys's murder, the pain of no longer having her with us feeding an increasingly frantic need to have answers. Fear of the unknown, no matter what we did, stayed present like a shadow. The presence of evil unbound remained close.

The other dimension, more tangible, immersed us in a life of compassion for others. We spent more and more time with bereaved parents and the poor. Our work with the local chapter of The Compassionate Friends had become an important part of our lives. We were primarily responsible for keeping the chapter going, hoping to give it momentum. We spent more time with people involved with the conflicts in El Salvador, where people were being murdered without anyone being brought to justice. To say "You can't do that to them" isn't enough for Fran or me anymore. We learned we must say "You can't do that to us" in order to be effective agents of change. When one hurts, all in solidarity hurt, and when one includes oneself in the group of victims, one gains authority to demand a response.

In addition to visits with our surviving children at Christmas, we went to the cemetery to visit Marlys's grave. Fran stood for a while, then bent to clear snow and pick dead leaves from the perennials she had planted. Winter doves were cooing, and the sun felt warm.

As we left the cemetery, the radio played a song from the 1950s, "At the Hop," by Danny and the Juniors. Fran and I had been planning to see the group on the day Marlys was attacked. "Remember? We were going to see them," I said, pointing to the radio.

After a long silence, Fran answered, "What do you think is the significance of that song playing now?"

"Coincidence," I offered.

"I don't believe in coincidence," she replied.

"I don't either. Let's say it's a sign we should live a long and happy life together, as we planned before Marlys's murder, as she wanted us to do. Let's say we heard this song because she still wants us to be happy, as long as we stop by to see that the grave is cared for."

"Then let's be happy," Fran said, "for a long, long time."

In July, quite unexpectedly, Sheriff Jim Frank called Fran to say they were running a major publicity program as part of the push to solve the crime. Could she help? Lynn had been asked to participate in a news conference but declined, not feeling confident about speaking to reporters. We didn't hesitate to get a ticket to Minnesota for Fran. How could she pass up this opportunity?

Washington County and the BCA cold case unit had begun to publicize the case, hoping someone would come forward. Fran met with Everett Doolittle, then with Sheriff Frank. The BCA had added $30,000 to the $10,000 reward offered by KSTP television and the $10,000 Fran and I had offered. A press conference gave the law enforcement agencies a forum in which to announce the increased reward. Fran had an opportunity to plead with the public to come forward with new information.

As Fran walked to join Frank at the microphone in the press room of the Washington County sheriff's office on July 31, 1996, she felt the full weight of the past seventeen years. She looked directly at the television cameras and began her plea. "Please help me find the person who murdered my daughter," she said. "Don't protect a murderer. If you know something, please, please tell us, whatever it is." She wiped away some tears, unashamed at the emotion she displayed.

While Fran waited for questions, Frank explained that he had formed an elite team solely for the purpose of solving this murder, and his efforts were being bolstered by a $50,000 reward.

Captain Mike Johnson looked at Fran. The veteran cop flinched at how painful it was for her. At the time of the murder, he knew Fran, knew Marlys, and was patroling their neighborhood as a deputy. He watched the reporters and camera crews, sensed excitement in their questions. This new team, which he would lead, had fresh information in the case, and for the first time it focused on a particular suspect, Joseph Donald Ture Jr. But without a collaborating witness, the case would never be solved.

A deputy waved Johnson to a telephone. Loen Kelly, a producer for the CBS television show *48 Hours,* was on the line.

"I just heard about this case," Kelly said. "We're really interested. We want to interview the mother." Johnson motioned Fran to him, whispering in her ear. "I'm on the line with a producer for *48 Hours*. They want to interview you. Are you willing to go on the show?"

"I'll do anything," she answered. "Just tell me what to say. I want Marlys's killer in jail." Taking the phone, Fran told Kelly, "I'd be happy to talk, but I'm supposed to be leaving for home tomorrow."

"We'll be there," Kelly said. "Today."

After she hung up, Fran turned to Johnson and said, "Good Lord, maybe something really can happen."

After the conference, Doolittle and Johnson took Fran into a small conference room where Sheriff Frank offered encouragement, then left to take care of other business. "You did great," Doolittle said, smiling at her. He knew the case had little hope of success unless some key witnesses came forward, and Fran's aura in front of the press seemed to project the combination of pathos and strength that just might motivate someone to call.

Johnson wanted to bring Fran up to date. So did Doolittle. "Fran," Johnson said, his expression showing his concern for her, "the focus of the investigation has centered on one individual, Joseph Donald Ture Jr."

"Ture?" she said. "And the alibi?"

"That's been rechecked," Johnson said. "We didn't do a good job back then. We called the Ford plant but didn't follow through with documentation. When we sent someone to the plant last month, we found out that the Joseph Donald Ture working that shift was Joe's father. He's the one who was actually at work at Ford on May 8."

"His father?" Fran asked, her swirling emotions tossing anger, disappointment, confusion.

Doolittle spoke up. "Joe Junior worked the night shift. We searched his papers and found a pile of pay stubs for many weeks, all for the second shift. It's interesting that we found stubs on both sides of the critical week. That one stub for the week of the murder was missing."

"What else wasn't done?" Fran said, sinking back in her chair, then leaning forward. "And what's being done with this task force? Are you using the same people who dropped the ball before?"

"Fran," Johnson said, "we know we screwed up back then. The new sheriff is going to put everything on this case that is needed. My team has new eyes and old eyes. I've assigned an investigator to the case full time. And Richter. They'll work together."

"Why Richter?" Fran asked. "Isn't he the one who didn't write reports? Isn't he the one who came in, had coffee with Boyden, sat there while Boyden lied to me about working the case every day? When I came in with Jack to meet Sheriff Frank, Boyden wouldn't even meet my eyes. I saw him at the restaurant and he avoided me."

"Calm down, Fran," Doolittle said. "Washington County is putting its best resources on the case. What's past is past."

"I hope you can see that, Fran," Johnson added. "I've told Richter and everyone else on the team that we aren't interested in blaming people. Nobody has to apologize for not writing a report. They just have to dig in now, find the old witnesses, check out leads. Richter is helpful. He remembers a lot about the case."

They talked for a while more, then Doolittle took a call from Loen Kelly, setting the time she would meet with him and with Fran later in the day. With that opportunity at hand, the three began to plan how to tell the story most effectively, how to use the media to create sympathy for the case without tarnishing Marlys's dignity.

After lunch in Stillwater, Doolittle took Fran to her old home in Afton where the murder took place. Two television crews went along, filming for the evening news.

Kelly called to ask Fran to meet her at a hotel in downtown St. Paul. "Let's find a place that is serene for tomorrow morning," Kelly said. Doolittle took them to Como Park, where Kelly and Fran talked for quite a while. As the two women sat at a picnic table, Kelly made notes that she would use to brief the production team. A trim, attractive woman who projects sensitivity and intelligence, Kelly drew Fran out softly, asking precise questions, sensing the way the story would be told. She felt that Fran made a good story—even better than the more documentary-style show she had originally planned, focusing on the BCA cold case unit. Here was an actual case. CBS could be part of the team. Kelly and Fran agreed that a CBS crew would come to Pennsylvania to allow Fran to make the appeal for help from her own home.

14

Who Was Watching

*O*N AUGUST 12, 1996, a CBS crew arrived at our house in Pennsylvania to interview Fran for the *48 Hours* fall season premier show. Erin Moriarity, the reporter who would interview Fran, listened to her talk about Marlys, asking questions, forming the dialogue in her mind. The camera crew went about their work of setting up, taking directions from producer Loen Kelly. All of them were gentle with Fran, realizing their questions would probe emotional wounds. We could see that Moriarity understood Fran's feelings. This professional team worked together—performed, really—setting everything up for later editing. During a moment of changing camera angles, Kelly mentioned to Fran that she liked our lifestyle, in spite of the grief.

The interview was painful but powerful. After some conversation, the cameras would stop and Kelly would ask questions, suggest directions for the discourse. The camera crew shifted from Fran to Moriarity and back during these breaks. The camera operator seemed to sense when to zoom in on Fran, when to give distance. They went upstairs to the landing at the top of the spiral staircase, looking at the memorials to Marlys, the antique third-grade school desk she fell against, the doll she had as a child.

At the end of the session, while the crew began to pack up, Fran laughed and said to Kelly and Moriarity, "I want you to promise me that when we solve this case, you'll film me without tears."

"That's a promise," Kelly said.

After they left, Fran and I, beleaguered and drained, slumped into our chairs, totally exhausted from the filming session. Thoughts and half-formed questions swirled in our heads, formed spoken questions with no answers. Had Fran said the right things? Would her appeal reach the ears of someone who knew something? What clue would be the key to solving the case, to an indictment and a conviction? Was there hope now?

On September 12, 1996, we and a whole lot of other people in the United States watched the *48 Hours* show. We clapped at Fran's tearful plea for someone to help solve the case. "I don't want to wait another seventeen years for justice," she had said. Several photographs of Marlys let a whole country see the pretty victim. Also in the segment were interviews of some of her friends, people who knew her and still cared about her. We were fascinated to see so much we didn't know.

Joe Ture also had a chance to talk. In an interview in the prison, Erin Moriarity asked him, point blank, "The police think you did it. Joe, what do you have to say to that?"

Ture smirked, then replied, "Let 'em prove it."

After the show, Fran and I watched the videotape we had made, again and again. We were now at the mercy of the viewers. Who would call?

Ray Lumsden sat with some other inmates in the Ramsey County Correctional Workhouse in St. Paul. In for violation of a no-contact order, the young man had been in and out of jail since he was a juvenile. He glanced at the television, picking up interest when the reporter began talking about a cold-case murder investigation. He saw the mother and her tears. They were talking about Afton, Minnesota, and the name struck a bell. When he saw a photo of Joe Ture, the prime suspect in the case, Lumsden jumped. "I know him," he said. "I remember he told me he killed someone in Afton."

Life was suddenly much more complicated. Lumsden knew the rules. It's dangerous to "rat" on fellow convicts. But he also understood that someone who would kill an eighteen-year-old high school girl has crossed a line. He called his girlfriend's mother. Lumsden had been trying to straighten out his life, relying on her for advice on how to stay out of trouble. "What should I do?" he pleaded, knowing the phone call was monitored. "Do the right thing," she answered. Still not sure, Lumsden talked to a correction officer who had become his friend.

Lumsden thought back to the St. Cloud prison, nine years before, when he was just seventeen years old. Both he and Ture worked in the diversified workshop, where they did woodworking projects. They weren't close, hanging with different cliques, eating at different tables. One time, when Lumsden had teased Ture about his bragging, Ture picked up a tool and waved it at the young man. "I went to a house in Afton and killed a young guy with one just like this," he said. Lumsden remembered the fear he felt then. What should he do?

He finally wrote a three-page letter describing his conversation with Ture. A few days later, Sergeants Klarich and Richter came to the jail to interview him. He repeated his story of Ture claiming to have killed a young man. He said he wasn't sure he could testify because he was concerned about ratting on another prisoner. "People lie in jail," Klarich said to Lumsden.

"I know, man. But this is too much. That Ture. You know, I could hit Ture's buttons every time."

"He got mad?" Klarich asked.

"Yeah. Real mad. It was entertainment, I thought. I'm a kid and I'm hanging out with others like me who know everything. So I called Ture a pedophile and he got really upset then."

"What did Ture do?" Klarich asked.

"One time he shouted, 'I've killed other people and I will

kill you' or something like that. He threatened me. But he also said it was a guy he killed."

"He threatened you?"

"Yeah. He held up a—I still don't know. Would be—it was a hatchet. About that long," Lumsden said, holding his hands apart to show the size, "and one side is a blade and the other side is like a—I think of it as a hammer, reverse side of a hammer. The thing had a blade on one side and two things on the other side like a two-grooved claw for pulling out nails or stuff."

Ray Lumsden finally agreed to testify. Having seen Fran on television, he felt compelled to come forward.

Also watching television that day was Dave Hofstad, the former deputy sheriff of Sherburne County, who found himself whirling back in time to the days when he worked with the county attorney. He vividly recalled sitting down with Ture during the Diane Edwards murder trial, before Ture was convicted. Acting on a tip from a reporter, he had asked, "Did you know the Wohlenhaus girl?"

Ture seemed content, even eager, to talk. He smirked as he answered, "I knew her. I had dated her, or tried to date her. I was able to get in her home. We talked. We argued. I killed her."

My God, Hofstad thought, coming back to the present, hasn't this case been solved after all these years? Hofstad had left law enforcement and now worked with a partner in a floor-covering company. He vowed his story would be heard this time. His partner was the father of another murder victim, and Everett Doolittle had helped convict Jamie's killer. Hofstad knew Doolittle and couldn't wait to make the call.

Twelve days later, Hofstad and Doolittle met at the BCA offices, taping their conversation. Hofstad said that Ture told him he had used a hatchet to strike down Marlys. Later, when he reviewed the transcript, Hofstad would cross out the word *hatchet* and put *crowbar* in its place.

Hofstad remembered writing a one-page report on a yellow legal pad. Doolittle asked the Sherburne County sheriff's office to search for the report. When Hofstad left the sheriff's office in February 1982, he had taken only his personal belongings. The office where Hofstad worked was temporary in those days, and his position had been filled by at least three others during the fourteen years that followed. The notes, for whatever reason, could not be found.

Others who were watching this show had equally horrified reactions. Tamera Hartman recognized Joe Ture as the man who kidnapped and raped her in a St. Paul garage two months after Marlys's murder. Donette Rico shuddered as she remembered being kidnapped and raped in October of that year, before finally escaping naked to a nearby house. Rosemary Stone recalled her narrow escape after being kidnapped by this man, who let her go when she falsely claimed she was pregnant. Cheryl Ann Korwes, Rosalie Sundlin, and more than a dozen other women shouted in horror when they saw Ture's image. "I know that bastard," they all said. "He raped me." The calls were pouring in.

A few days later, I left work early, walking the three-fourths of a mile home as usual. Halfway there I met Fran coming slowly toward me. She said, "The police are going to the grand jury in the first week in December. They have many corroborating testimonies pointing to Joseph Ture Jr. as the one who killed Marlys. They're going to indict him for Marlys's murder."

I was speechless, feeling relief, fear of the unknown, anger, joy, and confusion. We were living a replay of all the wondering. Somehow we made it home, though neither of us remembered the walk.

"What does it mean to say we're going to the grand jury?" Fran asked. "When he called, Everett [Doolittle] said Ture is a serial killer who noticed Marlys at a young adult hangout, then followed his pattern, being rejected when he tried to date her at the restaurant, ending up at her house to kill her. Marlys had a confrontation the Friday before the murder."

"Have they proved that?" I asked.

"No, they haven't proved it was Ture, yet, but it is possible. Everett thinks that Ture asked her to have sex in exchange for dope, like the confession says, and she had him tossed out by the manager."

"So this part of his confession is true, but displaced in time back four days to the Gene Daniels Restaurant."

"Then what?" Fran asked. "After three days of following her, he shows up at the house and kills her?"

"Right," I replied. "No conversation, no rape, just a violent serial killer who had nothing on his mind but murder for those who didn't fulfill his fantasy."

Fran spent half an hour on the phone with Captain Mike Johnson of the Washington County sheriff's office. Was Ture just a stalker, or was he a serial killer? Johnson couldn't say. Fran wondered if she would be strong, and would the man confess? Or will we be vulnerable and will he flaunt the crime at us? Johnson cautioned Fran, saying, "You and Jack need to look out for each other all of the time."

When we arrived in Minnesota in December, we stayed for a few days at Lynn's home, playing with grandchildren, talking with Lynn and her husband, Jay. The good family time gave us strength. KSTP-TV had a news spot at 5:00 p.m. on the grand jury. The next day Fran would start the process of confronting and indicting Marlys's murderer. We moved to a motel in Stillwater, close to the courthouse and an hour from Lynn's safe home.

So many times Fran had come to the Washington County complex, visiting the law enforcement officers, looking for help. Every time she went to Minnesota for so many years, she would sit at Undersheriff Boyden's desk and ask, "What's going on?"—and nothing was being done. In July, when Fran had participated in the press conference that got the evidence steamroller in action, she also went to the sheriff's building. This day was different. The wind and cold of December in Minnesota tugged at us as we walked across the open area from the sheriff's office to the courthouse and the prosecution branch of the county's legal system. In the county attorney's office were those who would represent the people of Minnesota against the "one or several persons" who had killed a human being in violation of the state statutes.

On the walk over, I said to Fran, "The county attorney represents the state."

"What are you saying?" she asked.

"Bluntly? They don't represent you. Or Marlys."

"Of course they do. They're going after Marlys's killer."

"Absolutely right," I said, "but they're doing it for the county and the people of Minnesota. We—you as the mother—are not the clients."

"Why are you telling me this?" she asked.

"I'm nervous. I'm a lawyer and I know what our kind do."

"I don't understand," she said, bracing herself against a blast of wind as we approached the courthouse door. "But I don't have to. That's your job. Protect me." In we went, down the hall, up in the elevator, into the offices of the county attorney.

After a briefing and time for Fran to ask questions, John Fristik, assistant county attorney, showed us the pictures of the crime scene he was going to use to illustrate the location where the killer struck down Marlys. Fran spent two hours reconstructing the room from the photographs, commenting, identifying, crying a bit. The staff watched patiently. We didn't learn much else about the case because grand jury hearings must be kept secret. We didn't even know the identity of any other witnesses.

Finally Fran's time to testify arrived. She went inside, glancing back at me with a quick smile, focusing on her task. I sat at a desk, trying to relax. How does one have a coherent thought when one's wife is being interrogated by a grand jury? What is it like for her, telling her story, a mother whose daughter was murdered? How does one ask for help? Perhaps a bereaved parent can, on some occasions, turn to the justice system.

A grand jury hearing is like a call of accountability, determining if a crime has been committed. It also decides if there is probable cause to charge one or more individuals with that crime.

Fran testified all afternoon and found release. When she finished, she met with an enthusiastic Sheriff Frank. County Attorney Dick Arney offered his support, telling her he had high praise for the lawyers he had selected to handle Marlys's case.

Now came reorientation, getting back to a role of waiting, wondering, sitting on the side. Fran tossed and turned all night until she made some sense out of her feelings. Confrontation is not the way to solve problems; dialogue and an exchange of points of view is more appropriate and offers dignity to each person involved. Sunday we went to church, where the sermon advised the congregation to accept what they couldn't change, change what they could change, and have the wisdom to know the difference. It's an old thought, too simple to do easily, but with hard work this well-known, even shopworn advice reaffirmed what Fran and I call the principles of accompaniment—The Compassionate Friends concept—as the way to resolve conflict. The two of us would watch, now on the sidelines, accompanying each other through the trial. We too would weigh the evidence, discuss the issues, avoid confrontation between ourselves or with others in the family over this case.

A day later, on December 23, the Washington County district attorney filed a true bill in the grand jury. Joseph Donald Ture Jr. had been indicted for first-degree and second-degree murder. At the press conference, Fran sat with Sheriff Frank and Dick Arney. Television crews filmed the announcement and ran pictures of Ture being brought into court.

After Christmas, we returned to Pennsylvania, where my three children and their families expressed relief from the long time of not knowing what really happened. Fran called other relatives and friends. We told everyone we knew, not quite stopping strangers in the street. In one way, the indictment ended a long period of waiting. Fran felt good knowing the probable murderer sat in jail awaiting trial. Meanwhile, she and I tried, not always successfully, to get back to a more routine life. On a blustery wintry day I raced home when Fran called in a panic over a window blowing open—an echo of that fateful day when she called me after finding Marlys dying. Neither of us was able to function much for the rest of the day. We had a glass of wine with dinner, read for a while, then went to bed early. It turned out to be a good cure.

Another night when Ray joined us at dinner, Fran observed how love and understanding beget and reinforce each other. Ray proposed an image of bereaved people being like a collection in a glass jar. "We don't know we're in one," he said, "and can't see the butterflies, who represent the children, the siblings, who have died, flying around outside the jar." Where else do people talk about the butterflies outside a glass jar? Where do they talk about love and understanding?

As a lawyer who had been involved in some litigation—civil matters relating to patents, not crimes—I knew trials were unpredictable. I didn't have any experience in criminal matters, however, and I wanted some level of confidence in the team Washington County had assembled. Would they be good enough to convict, if the evidence warranted it? I wanted to know what defense lawyers looked for, how they found holes in the prosecution's case. I've often said that the plaintiff has to win every issue, while the defense only needs one.

Through some contacts, I located Leonard Weinglass, a famous lawyer based in New York City. Many of his clients made national headlines. His reputation was extraordinary, and, to our delight, he agreed to see Fran and me.

On a nice April day, we took the train from Philadelphia to New York for the meeting. We entered a Lower Manhattan building, took the elevator to his floor. Weinglass greeted us as we pushed open the heavy metal door, welcoming us to his office and apartment. He was pleasant, reserved, and gracious as he led us to a large blue leather 1960s corner couch. He sat across from us in a patchwork wingback chair, a worn antique table between us cluttered with books.

Fran explained the case, giving as much detail as she could. Weinglass listened, asked a few questions. It became clear that he saw problems for the prosecution and opportunities for the defense. "You have no murder weapon, no eyewitness," he said.

The defense would try to raise a reasonable doubt, he said. Did the suspect have an unusual boot or shoe matching a print at the scene? One main issue in the case would be the admissibility of evidence. Where there aren't clear, tight, cleanly proven facts, prosecutors sometimes expand the case to get in more evidence, as though quantity might make up for lack of quality. "As a defense lawyer," he said, quoting another attorney, "I never win a case; the prosecutors lose them."

When prosecutors move into areas of conflict where facts aren't solidly provable, the whole house of cards can collapse, Weinglass cautioned. And he cautioned about so many confessions. "Be careful," he said. "Expanding the number of witnesses may bring in a bad one, not as credible. Cases get an aura, and it's possible for one character lacking good moral repute, who is not reliable, to hurt the whole case. Sometimes the bad ones taint the case. Defense lawyers are like a pack of hyenas who attack the weakest one in the herd. Find out if there is a questionable witness, with mental health history, drugs, crime. The defense will build their case on this one person." He warned us to look for any instance where the person receiving the confession benefited, by a transfer, a better job, any change in status, even a money payment. The defense would undermine the credibility of witnesses by showing they were getting something in exchange for the confession.

"Where are the weaknesses?" Weinglass summed up. He told us of another attorney who represented New York mob bosses who wrote on the outside of the file, "Where is the _____? What is missing?" "When he finds the answer and fills in the blank, he's ready to defend. Remember, defense lawyers never win a case; the prosecutors lose them."

15

Did You Know the Wohlenhaus Girl?

FRAN KEPT IN TOUCH with the prosecutors during 1997 while they built their case. They believed Ture raped and killed girls who reminded him of his first great but unrequited love, who had jilted him and had a child by another man. We were told that Ture assaulted her in 1976, putting a knife to her throat. They also told us about a woman who aborted Ture's child after he beat her and punched her in her stomach. Other conversations with the team working the case gave us additional bits and pieces of what seemed to be a growing pile of evidence. Meanwhile, we would have to wait.

In the ordinary part of our lives, Fran began our spring work in the yard while she waited for action on the trial. She talked about gardening, which affected her philosophy of life: "There is a spirit in every gardener. We try to bring beauty to everything we do. Sometimes we succeed and sometimes fail, but it doesn't matter. We have done something we believe in—taken a risk—striving for a fantasy of buds, blossoms, beauty. No gardener plants other than to the best of her ability. We have in our mind the right way. We might try new ways as each becomes a lesson. We aren't defeated but learn something each time."

When she talked like this I found it possible to see how she accepted life, most of the time, taking it all as it came. We had both tried—not with total success, by any means—to live well and to live for others, combining a life of culture and travel with a ministry of accompaniment. That summer, particularly, we labored and relaxed in our secret garden during the warm weather and tended to our different collections in the house all year, as a testimony to—if not a museum of—our activities.

May 8 came, another anniversary of Marlys's death. We bought landscape blocks to finish the back fence border. We tried to have a good day, placing the blocks in line, moving dirt to an herb garden, cooking a steak on the grill. More than usual, I felt serene, having gardened nearly all day. I dug dirt, loaded it, hauled it, unloaded and spread it, moved rocks, fixed borders and fencing. When we finished, I told Fran, "I am happy when I see the look on your face after a day of gardening."

Fran tried to be at peace that spring, knowing we were going to be involved on June 30 with an omnibus hearing to determine what evidence would come in and what would be kept out. One day we drove through the countryside, proving to ourselves once again that it is silly to have any car other than a convertible. We stopped at the cemetery to prune and tend flowers on Marlys's grave. It was our last piece of business in Pennsylvania before driving to Minnesota. Soon Fran would be in court, finally able to see the person charged with killing Marlys.

"Marlys wanted me to be happy," Fran said.

"I know," I encouraged, waiting for more.

"How can I be happy without being able to see her and touch her?"

"I don't know. Maybe that's why we come to the cemetery, to be in touch with something tangible, to feel."

"The last card I received from Marlys was at Easter, just before she was murdered. She signed it 'with love' and added a message. She wrote 'Be Happy,' and her words still ring clear today. More than anything, Marlys wanted me to be happy."

"No question," I said. "I remember Easter, too."

"It was an extremely difficult time in my life, going through a divorce, moving out of the house. Marlys saw my pain, and many times she said, 'Mom, it's okay. We'll be okay. Be happy.'"

"Can you do that? For her?"

"Yes. I can be happy, when I remember Marlys."

We were early, naturally, anticipating the opportunity to confront the person who confessed to killing Marlys. We went first to the sheriff's office, had coffee again with some of the investigators. They would be testifying over the next few days. We all went to the county attorney's office, again crossing the open space between arrest and conviction, now in the warmth of summer. In the hallway, we met the prosecutor pushing his cart full of files and documents, then followed him to the courtroom where the hearings would be held.

Outside were others, strangers to us, persons whose names were a jumble. Special Agent Doolittle introduced us to a girl who had been assaulted by Ture in Hudson, Wisconsin, just across the river, years before Marlys was attacked. She had picked him out on television, on *48 Hours*. We talked to the ex-con to whom Ture had confessed in jail in 1981 and who had written the three-page confession we so long ago had reviewed.

The judge's bench dominated the right side of the courtroom, facing down from the corner to give a view of the tables where the prosecution and defense sat and also facing the empty jury box. Spectators had two rows of seats on either side of the center aisle. We claimed the seats closest to the door where the defendant would enter and leave the courtroom.

Jeffrey Degree, a defense counsel, set up his materials, opening files, laying out papers, studying notes. He would make their opening statement. His co-counsel, Patricia Zenner, pranced in and out of the room, making last-minute calls and verifying loudly to her associate that Ture had been brought over from the jail. Prosecutor Rick Hodsdon also arranged his papers. The intensity of our emotions climbed with each new character taking his or her place on the stage.

Lynn and Jay arrived, taking seats with us. Becky, Beth, and Denise, Marlys's three faithful friends, sat behind us, reassuring Fran that the day had come. I looked over the whole room, holding on to the rail separating me from the path Ture would take. Nothing seemed real anymore.

After the clerk announced the judge, the Honorable Gary R. Schurrer, and called court into session, the door to my right opened. Ture walked into the courtroom, dressed in slacks and a white shirt open at the collar, not in the prison uniform I expected. He looked directly in our eyes, mine first, then looked quickly at Fran, then Lynn, Jay, the women behind us. He shuffled as he walked, dragging leg irons, and held his cuffed hands in front of him. Two solidly built deputies accompanied him, sitting behind and next to him, just out of earshot when he and his defense counsel whispered. Ture sat comfortably, patiently, not reacting much, not stoic but more unaffected by the proceedings. I wondered if, since he had been convicted of murder once, this proceeding posed little threat to him. He wasn't going anywhere soon, no matter what happened here.

How does one describe the person who is accused of, even indicted by a grand jury for, murdering one's child? He had the usual number of arms, legs, eyes, and other human attributes; he didn't look like a monster. His muscle had turned to fat, his hair early balding, his complexion sallow as one expects after fifteen years in prison. During the hearings, we learned that he liked candy bars and used large quantities of antacids. For two and a half days, I watched him sit impassively, not looking at me anymore as he shuffled in and out of the courtroom. I saw him glance at Lynn and other pretty women. Based solely on how his appearance struck me, undoubtedly a prejudiced view, I saw him as someone who had killed, had no remorse, and would kill again if somehow he was given his freedom.

At the beginning of the hearing, the judge and the lawyers for both sides had a conference. Judge Schurrer granted the defense motion to remove anyone from the courtroom who would be called to testify during the trial, a ruling almost always granted. But the immediate family would be allowed to stay, even if they would be testifying. We would hear the evidence against the man charged with murdering Marlys, striking her down in anger and premeditation. The other witnesses would not. We said good-bye to very unhappy friends of Marlys, excluded from the hearings because they were potential witnesses. We were the lucky ones. The judge, in his discretion, had seen fit to rule in favor of our request.

We listened to the opening statements by the defense and the prosecution, making notes but not having enough information to understand the substantive issues. Because grand jury proceedings are secret, we didn't know who the witnesses would be until each one began to testify. Much of what they said seemed out of context because the lawyers had the script and we didn't.

Near the end of the first day, a lawyer who had been Ture's public defender when Ture was convicted of murdering Diane Edwards in 1981 testified. Now a district judge, he "remembered the case well but said he couldn't really recollect, with certainty, having given permission to a deputy to speak with his client." He recalled his client talking with anyone who would listen. He wasn't quite sure of the circumstances about which he was being questioned.

I couldn't listen to this attorney with the dispassionate impartiality of a juror. But I didn't want to convict someone who wasn't guilty, any more than I wanted this defendant to go unpunished if in fact he was the murderer. I had been evaluating the witness, testing his words and the appearance of truth in what he said, how he said it. His testimony was filled with "it's probable that" or "I see no reason why I wouldn't have" and other imprecise wording that spoke to me of unwillingness to answer the questions fully. He didn't lie, of course, but his responses and demeanor, perhaps covering up what might have been his mistake, his duty to a former client, prompted me to say to Fran, "Here is another reason why people don't like lawyers."

The second day provided a powerful contrast to the jumbled puzzle pieces presented so far. Dave Hofstad identified himself as a former deputy sheriff and former acting sheriff of Sherburne County who worked with the county attorney during Ture's trial for the murder of Diane Edwards.

Quietly Hofstad told his story of being absorbed by law enforcement, not happy having to associate with criminals and evil deeds, trying to do his best. He recalled a phone call on Thanksgiving 1981, during the Edwards trial, from a television news reporter. The reporter asked him to talk to Ture about the Wohlenhaus case and about the town of Afton where Marlys lived and died. Hofstad first went to the county attorney, who sent him to Ture's public defender, who in turn told him he could talk to Ture about anything other than the Edwards case.

Our witness (we quickly claimed him for our own) went on to describe how he had Ture brought to a conference room in the jail, then sat down with him, just the two of them. Hofstad read the Miranda warning to Ture and told him he could leave immediately or at any time if he wanted to stop the conversation. Ture, he said, seemed content, even eager, to talk.

Then Hofstad asked Ture, "Did you know the Wohlenhaus girl?"

Hofstad testified that Ture answered, "I knew her. I had dated her, or tried to date her. I was able to get in her home. We talked. We argued. I killed her."

Hofstad couldn't remember if Ture had said he used a crowbar or a hatchet but did recall Ture specifically saying he used one of those two weapons. At that moment, Hofstad said, Ture stopped talking, saying only that the interview was over.

Even though this was only an evidentiary proceeding, one of many in the omnibus hearings, even if a jury would still have to hear this and other testimony both for and against the

issues, we had now heard his confession. How could a reasonable doubt exist? The witness seemed so reliable, so believable,
so without any motive not to tell the truth.

Hofstad went on to say that he had called Washington
County the same day he talked to Ture and left word with the
sheriff's office of an important break in the Wohlenhaus case.
No one ever returned his call.

I asked Fran, "How can I be so stupid as to be surprised by
this testimony?"

She wasn't pleased either. "How could Washington County
law enforcement be so stupid? They had the killer in 1981. It's
1997!"

At a break, I hugged Fran, saying, "I think we've heard
the truth. Look at him." Dave Hofstad stood alone, not speaking with anyone during the time between direct and cross-
examination. Later, when we got to know him, we would find
him to be a solid Minnesota citizen, doing his job at the time
but fed up with the atrocities filtering through the system. He
followed the guidelines but ran away from further conflict. If
only he had pushed harder to make contact with Washington
County. There's no way of knowing if a receptionist lost the
message, or if Undersheriff Boyden ignored the call because
of Ture's supposed alibi, or if any number of other possible
reasons caused this lead not to go any further. Not until 1996,
when *48 Hours* caught his attention, did Hofstad come forward to tell his story, finally, to Washington County investigators. Why did he let it slide?

On cross-examination, Degree went over Hofstad's testimony, trying to suggest that the interview was improper, either
for lack of warning or because Hofstad didn't have proper
permission. As Hofstad consistently affirmed his testimony,
I wondered about the strategy; the cross-examination seemed
to be substantiating and confirming everything Hofstad said.
Finally, defense counsel asked the question, "Sir, how many
people have confessed murder to you?"

Hofstad looked at him. "Only one. The defendant. And that's why I remember it so clearly."

For the first time, I actually thought there was evidence to convict the murderer. What more did we need? The next witness was the one who caused all the excitement in 1981, claiming he had written down a confession that Ture signed. Toby Krominga told his story calmly, entertainingly, we hoped convincingly. First he and Ture fought, to establish the pecking order, Krominga said. Then they played cards and talked. Krominga quoted Ture as asking, "Would people think I'm crazy if I killed a bunch of people?" They developed a plan to write a letter in which Ture confessed to Marlys's murder, and to the murder of a family. They would send it to the judge and hope Ture would be sentenced to a better prison facility for psychiatric care.

We wondered how we could evaluate what Krominga said, knowing he had been convicted of various felonies, served time. Was he the one we should watch for, as our New York consultant had suggested?

Deputy Sheriff Jeff Klarich described how Washington County had prepared a photo identity procedure and showed it to a number of people. Klarich explained who each person was, told how and why they were selected, how the process had been designed to allow potential witnesses an opportunity to identify the defendant. A number of people had picked out Ture, each one placing him in the St. Croix Valley back in May 1979, contrary to his statements to investigators and the media.

Klarich spoke of one person who remembered having a drink in a bar across the road from the café where Marlys worked. This man had been asked by Ture for work and turned him down. When he left the bar, he found that his truck had been vandalized. That testimony certainly would put the defendant at the scene.

The last witness for the prosecution was Special Agent Everett Doolittle. He had interviewed Ture a number of times, not always with a Miranda warning until Ture again was a suspect. Dolittle testified that Ture voluntarily met with him and had the opportunity to leave at any time, though he never did.

The prosecution's case was completed, and now the defense would attack, I assumed. Defense counsel called Leon Dehen, a retired Sherburne County jailer who worked at the time Ture and Krominga wrote the confession during the trial in 1981. He remembered a different story from what we had heard. The witness told the judge that Krominga was working for one of the investigators, who he said needed a go-between, trying to get a confession for the county. Krominga would be rewarded with conjugal visits from his wife, perhaps even other favorable treatment. Was this the weak link, the "something" lacking in the case? Favoritism for this prisoner as he obtained a confession might act as a domino, destroying the credibility of all the confessions.

On cross-examination, prosecutor Rick Hodsdon asked Dehen if he had ever worked as an investigator. He had not. Had he had any contact with county personnel doing the investigation? He had not, even for that ongoing trial. Did he have any firsthand knowledge of cooperation between Krominga and any investigators? He did not; his only source of information was Krominga himself. Finally, he admitted that he had no reason to believe or not believe Krominga, other than that he did see Ture sign the confessions and assumed everything else Krominga said was true.

It wasn't a weak link after all. This testimony actually helped, corroborating the fact Ture signed each page of the confession after it had been written, contradicting what he told television reporters, that he had signed blank papers as part of a petition relating to prison food.

Now we would wait for the briefs to be filed and for the judge to rule on the admissibility of the evidence.

Part IV

Justice

16

In the Presence of Evil

ONE MORNING Fran woke up feeling sad about losing Marlys—and angry at Jim Wohlenhaus for leaving her in 1965, putting her on the path that led to her living in the house where Marlys died. As I got out of bed, Fran said, "If only I had not tried to be strong, I could have given up and gone back home to Virginia when Jim left me."

When we talked more at breakfast, Fran looked at me accusingly. "You know," she said, "you offered some sympathy this morning, then kissed me and left me crying as you went off down the hall to get ready for work. You don't understand my grief; if you did, you'd have done more."

I explained my version of the morning. The phone rang during my shower. Memory and panic flooded me, because I feared the phone call meant disaster. Did Fran have a premonition of a caller verifying some tragedy? It turned out to be harmless but provoked a reaction common to those who have known sudden grief: horror comes back abruptly. Are we to experience unbearable loss again? Can it happen again? Even when it's a false alarm, we struggle.

When we were visiting Minnesota while we were waiting for the judge to rule, Fran went alone to our bedroom at Lynn's house. The light was on and the thin curtains couldn't hide the shadows on the snow-streaked brush and brown grass. When

I came to bed, Fran said, "While you were in the kitchen reading, I felt fear again. I'm not this way in Pennsylvania."

Jay, our son-in-law, told us of a friend whose boss worked
at the St. Cloud prison when Ture talked about the multiple
murders he was suspected of committing. Fran said, "I wasn't
planning to work on the case, but I did call Everett."

"We're not," I replied. "This came to us. Hopefully Everett
will find that Ture mentioned a fact only the killer would
know." We always hoped for more evidence.

That evening a newscaster announced that a prisoner had
been killed in the Stillwater prison. It sounded like Ture's
name. Someone said, "I hope they killed him," and Fran
came running into the room. We then heard the victim was
not Ture but a man with a similar name. Fran said, "I'd just
as soon avoid the trial if I could. It's going to be too intense."
A second news story told of a Washington County sheriff's
deputy being attacked, and we watched Sheriff Jim Frank
being interviewed, saw deputies we knew in the background.

We couldn't relax in Minnesota because fear was always
lurking just below the surface, so we went back to Pennsylvania and waited. Three days short of what we had mentally
set as a deadline for the judge to rule, Fran called my office
from home. "Are you sitting down?" she said, tearfully. "Mary
called." Mary Waldkirch was the victim assistance coordinator
for Washington County. "She said the judge denied all of the
defense 'somethings' and the evidence will be admitted."

"Defense motions to suppress the evidence offered."

"Yes," she affirmed. "But the judge didn't rule yet on ad-
mitting the Spriegel cases."

I spoke calming words, unable to wipe her tears away over
the telephone. "Make a cup of tea," I suggested. "Call Lynn
and your sister. Call Marlys's friend Becky."

"I don't feel like calling right now. I'm drained."

"Then try to relax." We hung up.

Spriegel cases, named for a Minnesota Supreme Court

decision, are crimes and actions of the defendant that aren't directly relevant to the main case, offered by a prosecutor to show a pattern of conduct—a serial killer who always picks on young blond women who look something like his former girlfriend, say—or as evidence that he was in a certain place at a specific time. The courts want to avoid prejudicial evidence but will admit evidence of some wrongful acts when it can be used directly to prove an element of the crime for which the defendant is being prosecuted. Ture had bounced a check in a town he denied ever visiting. The prosecutors wanted to show he wrote the check in Afton and offered to exclude the insufficient funds charge.

A minute later Fran called again. "I forgot to tell you. Diane Edwards's father wants to talk to me. He's been following the case. He may even have been at the courthouse."

Five minutes later, Fran called once again. She had talked to her sister and to Becky. "Lynn wasn't home, and I didn't leave a message."

"Of course not."

The judge had set a schedule for a series of the Spriegel hearings. The prosecutors would present evidence of a series of rapes, then offer evidence that Ture killed Joan Bierschbach and, lastly, Alice Huling and three of her children. The night before we were to leave for our next confrontation with Marlys's killer, I dreamed of the monster of my childhood nightmares. In the dream I screamed at the Technicolor apparition, who grinned maliciously. Awakened in the dark of the night, I couldn't recall its name, but it is fear.

In the early morning, with the car loaded and ready, I sat on the patio as the dark left the sky. Doves cooed, birds chirped, distant traffic and our wind chimes gently tolled in the warm breeze. We were leaving this sanctuary to do battle with the devils, those out there and the ones within us. I imagined each of the seven rape victims identifying this man as her attacker, accusing him of the crime.

Both of us felt the tremendous weight of anticipation of the hearings. This enormous anxiety, much like the expectations before a birthday or anniversary of a death, is familiar to bereaved parents. But now it was not grief but evil we foresaw. Our Compassionate Friends colleagues told us that the events might not be as bad as we expected.

The morning the hearings began, we sat in the courtroom after talking with cops, lawyers, administrators, witnesses, and victims. I felt my lawyer training coming forward to help posture the case and keep our personal defenses in place. Weighing every word for potential harm or good to our cause, I kept close to Fran, advising her what to say when a question came up. Fran is good at taking my thoughts, putting them into her words, and using them effectively to meet the public. I felt neither outwardly observant nor inwardly reflective.

The first day absorbed us completely as two women testified about the violent actions of the man accused of murdering Marlys. Fran shuddered at their graphic descriptions. Ture colored slightly during enflaming testimony but otherwise sat quietly. At the lunch break, three television reporters interviewed Fran. She stood alone, her back to the courthouse hallway wall, surrounded by the media, speaking into each microphone in response to questions. She spoke of the women finally having the opportunity to confront the man who had assaulted them, of her own taking on the pain of these victims, and of her refusal to let hate consume her.

The reporters shifted to interview defense attorney Jeff Degree. I listened to him characterize issues and events most favorably for his client, doing his job. "Even the mother admits the confession contains inconsistencies," Degree said.

We met Donald and Bonnie Edwards, the parents of the young woman Ture had been convicted of murdering. I watched them stare intently at the person who took Diane from them.

Would we someday be like them, knowing who took a precious life from us? Were we already like them? Also in the courtroom were an uncle and two aunts of Joan Bierschbach, another murder victim. Next to me, Fran watched Ture, then followed the story of each witness as though memorizing the testimony.

The next day we had dinner with parents of a raped and murdered young girl who are active in Parents of Murdered Children. They were kind, offering advice about what we might expect to happen to us. We contrasted the advocacy of their group with the more healing philosophy of The Compassionate Friends. They wanted to talk about the "what-if's" plaguing both of them, and they appreciated our similar experiences. My heart nearly stopped when the mother told us they heard the man who raped their daughter say he killed her "because she had such sad eyes."

On the way home I said, "It would have been worse if Marlys had been raped, too."

"No," Fran replied, "it wouldn't. I've been very careful to tell people the death of a child is the worst. No matter how they die, nothing changes that. Death itself is the defining act, not the baggage coming with the particular death. I work very hard to keep people from comparing, like when someone says, 'It's worse for you because your child was murdered.' I tell them it's no different. The death of a child is so bad, there is no comparison possible between the ways a child dies."

I silently found relief that Marlys had not been raped. For me, it really would have been worse.

After a two-month adjournment, from April to June 1998, due to the judge's schedule, once again we prepared to confront Marlys's killer. At our motel near Stillwater, we tried to anticipate our reaction to the next few days. Seven women had looked the defendant in the eye and said, "You did this to me." Their testimony provided some sense of justice, at least allowing each victim to confront the one who committed this violence. Now, as we looked at a murder case as old as ours, we saw only this one difference. Joan Bierschbach wouldn't be able to say a word. The system and the witnesses would have to speak for her.

During the hearings, we were developing a rapport with the prosecutors. I remarked to Rick Hodsdon how an early starting time one day made us hurry, and he responded, "It's never too early for me. I love this stuff." A few minutes later, his co-counsel John Fristik came in, accidentally spilling some ice cubes he had brought to keep his drinking water cool. As he cleaned up the ice, defense counsel Jeff Degree picked up two cubes, putting them in his own glass. I had just witnessed a telling illustration of my profession: one lawyer taking advantage of another's mischance to his own benefit.

Hodsdon's opening statement said he would prove that Joan Bierschbach, a happy twenty-year-old, disappeared in November 1979 after encountering the defendant. Her body, found five years later, showed death by murder. In response, the defense attacked the credibility of the convicts who had heard Ture's confessions. Mudslinging began immediately, when the defense tried to show that Joan had suicidal impulses, banishing any doubt I had that we were in a war.

Joan Bierschbach's mother, Lorraine, sadly answered many questions with "I don't recall" or "I don't understand the question," and our hearts poured out to her. She had never done anything to try to solve the case or push the investigation. We learned later that she took great comfort simply in knowing her daughter hadn't taken her own life. Her solace, for now, lay in the corroboration we saw in court that day of her daughter's murder. Lorraine seemed paralyzed by courtroom events, going home after her testimony, not to return. Lorraine achieved peace by knowing where and how her daughter died, and by having her chance to rebut the lies of the defense. Perhaps this was all her strength permitted her to do.

Joan's boyfriend seemed wrapped in sadness as he talked about his long-ago girlfriend. Others—roommates, cops, investigators—each had a turn to testify, as Ture sat, head cocked to one side. In the calm, comfortable, nicely furnished courtroom, the word *murder* seemed out of place. The defense counsel tried to get issues of mental instability into the case, again an attempt to punish the victim or at least cast a shadow over her memory. Near the end of the day, Joan Bierschbach's brothers and sisters saw pictures of their sister's teeth; these were used to identify her. Like their mother, they too never came back.

During the testimony, I found myself looking at a factual dilemma. If Joan saw the defendant at lunch at a restaurant as one set of witnesses said, then visited with her two roommates, called her boyfriend, went to play volleyball, why didn't she say something about her fear? Fran reminded me that Ture had a pattern of meeting his victim, being rejected, then after thinking about the harm he would do, coming back to kill her. Joan probably didn't suspect that he would abduct and kill her.

Day two of testimony in the Bierschbach hearing began with a detailed description of a young boy finding Joan's body. As we watched each item of clothing be identified, a crazy image of someone opening gifts came to mind. It was horrible, as if we were in hell celebrating evil. Ture grinned when a witness said the T-shirt wasn't white. Forensic evidence identified Joan's body—from bones and a few items of clothing. The cause of death, a stab to the chest, matched consistently with a hole in a sweater and cuts on the inside of two ribs.

Toby Krominga, now back in jail for theft by swindle, was a key witness because of his many conversations with Ture while they were in the same jail. In 1981, Ture told Krominga he had killed Joan Bierschbach, stabbing her in the chest. Her body, found in 1984, didn't reveal the cause of death until the very recent forensic autopsy work we had just heard. In the early 1980s, only the killer would have known exactly how she died.

Who killed Joan Bierschbach? How certain must we be? How much can be missing and still give a complete picture? This did not seem like a convincing case when we looked at it objectively. Fran and I talked about this imagery of a puzzle with some pieces missing. If we were looking at a landscape, some of the sky could be missing and we would still know the scene. If it's a murder, would we also have answers? We hoped in our trial, and in these hearings, there would be enough pieces we could believe that we could say the picture was clear. When we went to trial for Marlys's homicide, we would need as many facts as the prosecution could present.

The next witness, convicted felon Jeffrey Morris, testified about Ture telling him about the odometer noise in the victim's car; only the close family and the killer could have known about it. Morris certainly fit the criteria of a problem witness, misbehaving, acting out in an effort to get attention. Morris offered to hire the defense counsel to bring suit against the prison. Spectators and investigators in the courtroom laughed as this strange person testified. We were propelled from laughter, hearing a convict calling correctional officers retarded, to revulsion, at his testimony of Ture urinating in a dying woman's mouth.

Here was a dangerous witness, perhaps a foreshadowing of what we would hear in the case for killing Marlys. Three different convicts brought forth confessions Ture made, telling how Ture killed Joan. Did we need, and want, all three in Marlys's case?

When hearings began on the Huling murder case, I tried to imagine the reaction of the surviving son, Bill, who would be facing the killer of his mother and three siblings. I anticipated new witnesses, new faces mixing in with the regular cast. In the opening statement by John Fristik, we were told we would learn how and why Alice Huling and three of her children died, and how Billy survived. We would see and hear evidence linking the defendant to these murders.

Then came the evidence. Vivid, obscenely enlarged photographs of Alice Huling's nude, bloody body were held up for all to see. Once again, a victim's decency had been ignored. The prosecutor held up huge graphic depictions of horror, one after another. We were in a human slaughterhouse. I hesitated to look or to look away as the photographs were handed to the defense team for admission as evidence. Next came photos of sixteen-year-old Susie Huling, thirteen-year-old Wayne, and twelve-year-old Patti. A defense lawyer finally asked the prosecutor to offer them all at once, to reduce the waves of horror. By then I'd stopped looking at the exhibits. What had it felt like to see a weapon pointed at oneself, then die from the blast from the shotgun? How much time did each of the victims have? What thoughts went through their minds? No longer simply a story told by law enforcement officials or newspaper accounts, the events had become frighteningly vivid.

When Bill Huling testified, he told the court of the divorce that divided his family, giving details of his mother's work, his schooling and activities, putting the humanity back into his family. These were real people, not just the grisly remains of mass murder. He walked us through the final day, coming home from school, playing and doing homework, saying goodnight to his family. Then Bill told of the terror of being awakened by noises he described as muffled voices and wrestling coming from his mother's downstairs bedroom.

His brother Wayne said, "What was that?" and they heard more noise, followed by the sound of a gun being fired. Then they heard heavy footsteps coming up the stairs to the children's bedrooms. Bill described a man standing in the doorway, illuminated by a light at the top of the stairs. Wayne said, "Who are you?" The man shot Wayne in the head. Bill testified he heard the pump action of the shotgun, then his sister Patti saying, "What's going on?" The man replied, "It's okay. Go back to sleep," and then he shot her. Another pump of the shotgun, then half a scream from Susie and another round fired. The man came back to Billy's room, firing a slug round at the young boy hiding under his covers, barely missing him. The man poked him with the barrel and fired again when a breath escaped. This shot too missed Billy, but he didn't move when he was poked again. The roar of the barrel deafened him, and it took ten minutes for his hearing to return.

On cross-examination, the defense counsel tried to show how a family friend, a deputy sheriff living next door, could have been the man with the shotgun. Under ugly questioning, Bill firmly stated that he was sure the murderer wasn't the family friend, nor could it have been his own father, nor another man suggested by the lawyer. Throughout the questioning, witnesses had to respond to interrogation, putting the reputation or character of the victims into question. Each time we felt sad for the Huling family, also knowing our turn would come in Marlys's trial.

Bill Huling's testimony established facts, not feelings, to prove a murder had been committed. We listened to him describe being present when his mother and siblings were murdered, while he, scared unmercifully, lay under his sleeping bag. His surviving a night of terror had importance for the lawyers only for what he could tell the court. In contrast, Fran expressed compassion for Bill.

That night we joined Bill and some of the investigators at one of their homes for dinner. During the pleasant meal, I asked Bill how he could act so calm, show so little of what he must be feeling. "How have you adjusted so well?" I asked. He replied that he had been in intense counseling for several years and had faced the demons. Later, on our drive back to the motel, Fran asked me to drive by the cemetery at the church where Marlys's funeral was held. Only then did Bill talk about his family, about relationships and how they changed because of the murders.

The next day brought an astounding highlight. Prosecutor John Fristik finally asked Bill about the toy car found in Ture's car four days after the murders. "Have you found my Batmobile?" Bill asked, then testified in court that the car was just like the one he had played with the day of the murders.

Dr. Mike McGee, pathologist and chief medical examiner for Ramsey and Washington counties, gave his opinion that the metal club wrapped with steering wheel leather that had been found in Ture's car caused the blunt trauma to Alice Huling. The toy and the club were physical evidence linking the defendant directly to the scene of the homicides. The rest of the day found a host of witnesses coming forth to make clear the chain of custody on these two pieces of evidence.

The good feelings of making progress in the case dissipated with a scheduling problem, and the judge adjourned the hearing until August. The prosecution hadn't finished its case, and the defense hadn't even started to present its evidence.

17

Sick and Tired of Bad News

*T*HE HEARINGS IN STILLWATER, MINNESOTA, in April and June 1998 helped us to understand how many victims had not had closure—a word often used but seldom understood. A guilty verdict concludes the case but does not bring back a murder victim. We had heard testimony that tied Joe Ture to the murders of Joan Bierschbach and of Alice Huling and three of her children, with evidence only the murderer would know. We had met the parents of Diane Edwards, of whose murder Ture had been convicted. All of these families shared with us the tragedy of the death of a child. As we sat in the courtroom together, we all offered and received comfort; each of us understood how the others felt. It was important to know we were not alone.

Fran and I purchased a motor home to live in during the next set of hearings in August and for the trial later in the fall. This solved our logistical problems, and we would have a sanctuary for the evenings, after court, where we could be consoled by our two dogs.

We prepared the motor home for the trip, putting clothes in the closets, packing food in the cupboards, refrigerator, and freezer, and generally busying ourselves with getting ready to leave. Fran put a "care-bear" mascot in the front window. She decorated it with badge pins from support groups like Parents of Murdered Children and The Compassionate Friends and with gifts from Special Agent Everett Doolittle—badges representing the Bureau of Criminal Apprehension in Minnesota and, of course, the Washington County sheriff's office.

Standing in the kitchen putting away food, Fran talked about times with her children, wishing she could show this big RV to Marlys. Ray had seen it, and we were traveling to Minnesota where Lynn would see it. "What would Marlys think," she asked, "about what we have done so far to solve her murder?" Fran felt that Marlys would be proud of the work we had done and our efforts to keep the perpetrator from killing again.

The next morning, Fran excitedly told me of a dream, of Marlys coming to her as a young teen, bubbling with laughter. In her dream, Fran looked toward the large front window of the motor home, seeing Marlys standing on what appeared to be the bumper, looking in the window, waving, smiling her biggest smile. Fran saw a happy girl giving approval to her mom for what we were doing. Then the scene changed, and Marlys stood with Lynn and their grandfather—Grandpa Dave—and again Marlys waved happily.

Fran recounted every detail, cherishing the joy of the visit, a sign we were doing the right thing. She loved hearing "Mom, be happy" one more time. We later learned that four days after that dream, Grandpa Dave passed away, at the age of seventy-seven. Lynn had been visiting Grandpa Dave regularly at the hospital. We think that care of his spirit had been transferred from Lynn to Marlys.

Later we talked about going back to Minnesota. Fran said, "I look at the next few months as work yet to be done. Our family has been tormented for many years; when we go to trial it will have been more than nineteen years. There are answers we need and this will bring us to fruition. We're going as witnesses. We're going on a mission of accomplishment. We're going on a culmination of everything, not just since we decided to solve the case ourselves a few years ago. From day one we've wanted it solved. Our return from exile that projected us to solve the crime has now played out, the fruits of our labor. I don't think anyone understands how much work we put into solving the case."

At church the day before we started the drive, we were called up at the end of the service for a formal prayer and laying on of hands, to send us with strength for the mission ahead and, as our priest rightly said, to continue helping others in their grief. A woman read a line of Scripture: "Father, forgive them for they know not what they do." Fran was startled by the reading. "It's like we are being crucified," she said, "just like Marlys suffered a truly incomprehensible death."

We left the safety of our house to face an adversarial system aspiring to prove the guilt of Marlys's killer. We felt fear and recalled other trips. This time our focus was solely to accomplish our goal. We cut off relationships and ties to home—The Compassionate Friends, Romero Interfaith Center, Philadelphia Writers Organization, our church and its blessing, even my children. We were moving back to Minnesota, to survive this time. We weren't moving forever, just for as long as it would take to find justice. Focused on justice, we left nothing behind.

Many friends and acquaintances have said they couldn't imagine going through this kind of trial so many years after the crime. But we could imagine what it would be like. In 1979 we went through the murder, with all the pain and alienation. Now we would be living it again, as a multi-act play. The judge would be the director, staging the many characters in his courtroom, as witnesses presented bits and pieces of truth as they saw it from their perspectives. The action would be in slow motion, with prosecuting and defending lawyers editing the testimony, structuring the story for the jury. The most important personalities would be the two of us, and Marlys, who wouldn't come back to life no matter what the verdict. Fran and I would participate in a legally sanctioned re-creation of what we had lived with for over nineteen years. Then we would return home to live the rest of our lives.

Why should anything this significant be easy? As we started to leave, I broke an electrical plug for the motor home, then a trailer taillight didn't light up. We had a nearly dead battery, then a strap came off the car I towed. None of these little problems was difficult to solve, and we fixed each one as it came up, but the first night, as we sat outside the motor home in the evening breeze, I told Fran I was exhausted. I had trouble finding energy to do any little thing. She felt the same way, having slept during most of the day's drive, something she had never done before.

In Minnesota, we settled in where Washington County authorities had arranged for us to park our motor home. The first afternoon we spent installing a telephone line we expected to be waiting for us. Now the details of work seemed to relax us. Solving simple problems became therapy, not barriers.

September 14, 1998, marked the start of the trial of our lives. Would there be justice for Marlys? The first prospective juror spoke about knowing one of the key witnesses. She asked to be excused, saying she knew Ture was guilty. Ture started to cry. Perhaps reality had reached him, but be assured—no one had any sympathy for him.

He showed up the second day unshaven, in prison garb, missing his dental plate. The two defense attorneys argued that they couldn't work with him; he couldn't get a fair trial. They wanted him evaluated for mental health and his ability to present a defense. Judge Schurrer denied the motion and ordered an examination in such a way that the ongoing selection of jurors wouldn't have to stop. Then he told Ture he wouldn't let him sabotage the case. While we survived this scare, we realized that we had just experienced the first of the many "bad news" events we could expect. We remembered that "court is war."

The third day began on a difficult note. Prosecutor Rick Hodsdon had lost an election just two days ago, as he sought to be elected county attorney to replace Dick Arney, a good man who had died in office. As we waited for the judge, I offered sympathy, telling him of the day I lost temporary custody of my children during my divorce in 1978 and while I worked intensely in a trial in Washington, D.C. We talked about setbacks and continuing to strive toward our goals. He spoke fondly of the deceased county attorney, whom he considered his best friend and whose death inspired him to run for the office. We both knew that without the commitment of Dick Arney, a bereaved parent himself, and Hodsdon's own determination, we never would have come this far.

Minutes later the judge called for the lawyers to come to his chambers before the court session. The stage had been set for disaster; Fran and Joan Bierschbach's aunt both felt strange, even disoriented. I thought the judge could be ruling on the admissibility issues. His clerk had been more visible recently, as though the work he had been assigned came closer to completion. When the prosecutors came back, they weren't happy. "It wasn't what I expected," John Fristik said. "I'll talk to you later."

We sat in court, knowing only that Fristik had gone to see the acting county attorney for advice. Would important evidence be excluded? We listened vaguely to a prospective juror being questioned, not even smiling when she talked about getting a break from a judge on a speeding ticket. I said, half aloud, "I'm sick and tired of bad news."

We needed to hold on to the commitment we had made, not give up, knowing we were going to continue to seek justice in light of every bad decision we had to face. At the break we learned that the only other case coming in as Spriegel evidence would be the murder for which Ture had already been convicted, that of Diane Edwards.

Before we could adjust to the news, we learned that Fristik planned to ask the county attorney to dismiss the complaint, fearing he couldn't win the case. I heard him clearly, but Fran asked me, "What does he mean?" Blunt in my response, I told her, "John wants to drop the case and forget about the trial!"

To say we were devastated would be the understatement of the century. Fristik left, presumably going to his office. Hodsdon stayed with us, assuring us there would be no stopping, no giving up. Fristik simply had a bad reaction to the ruling. We could still win the case and he, Hodsdon, would take it on by himself if need be.

Dazed but assured, we met Everett Doolittle and his partner for lunch. They too were reassuring, but what did cops know? They left us for a meeting with the prosecutors, the county attorney, and others who would be making decisions. We drifted back to our motor home.

Several hours later Hodsdon called to say there had been no change in plans. "We're going ahead, and we think we have a good chance of winning. John will be on board and do a fabulous job. Just watch how we go at it."

We were unprepared for the case to collapse, not able to understand how the judge could rule for the defendant. The prejudice of the Huling family murder—according to the judge—outweighed the justice of stopping a serial killer even when the killer had been proven by clear and convincing evidence to have committed murder. He rejected the seven rape cases, saying they were "not related enough to Marlys's case." Evidence in the Bierschbach case, the judge found, really didn't support a finding of murder, in spite of the confessions. Almost none of what we had heard in April, June, and August would come into the trial. That evidence convinced us of his guilt; how did it serve justice to ignore it? How could society ignore what Ture had done?

Monday morning Fran held me close when we walked into the courthouse, not sure of what the legal system had done. We requested a meeting with the two prosecutors and the acting county attorney. I asked them what happened to the evidence we knew about—Ture hassling Marlys on the Friday before the attack, Marlys coming home Sunday night acting as though something had happened. When would we hear this evidence?

Hodsdon told us the only witness who could testify about Friday night was such a loose cannon they didn't want him on the stand. The Sunday-night event, Fristik said, happened on Monday according to the girlfriend who was with Marlys.

As I spoke to these lawyers, experts in criminal matters, much more knowledgeable about the rules of admissibility and the justice system in general, I could see myself struggling to say words that made sense. When I stopped talking, we all agreed to work hard, keep our nose to the grindstone, never give up. At least we were going to trial to start presenting the case against Joe Ture.

Judge Gary Schurrer began giving preliminary instructions, setting out rules under which the jurors were to focus on the facts, not on lawyer's arguments. First-degree murder required proof that the death occurred in Washington County, where the court had jurisdiction; that this defendant caused the death; that the defendant intended to kill; and that the murder was premeditated. There is no set time for premeditation; it can be short but not rash. All this must be proved beyond a reasonable doubt. If the other elements are proved without premeditation, the verdict should be second-degree murder. Both intention and premeditation may be inferred because mental state can't be known.

Reasonable doubt, the judge said, is "proof upon which reasonable persons would act in their most important affairs." I liked that definition, and the more I thought about it, the more hope I had of jurors acting on the proofs we had in Marlys's case. Her murder had been our most important affair; now it had to be theirs.

Fran and Ray were asked to leave during the opening statements, to prevent their testimony from being tainted by what the lawyers said to the jury. Lynn and I were there for the jurors to see.

Rick Hodsdon presented the case for the state of Minnesota. "It is a case of murder," he said and showed the jury an enlarged photograph of Marlys—the same photo that had been on her closed casket in 1979. He said the state would prove beyond reasonable doubt that the defendant, sitting there—he pointed—with premeditation and with criminal intent killed Marlys. The case would come in bits and pieces, putting together a complete picture.

He gave an overview for the jury. He told them the story of Marlys's murder in a straightforward manner, not hiding the horror of the attack. Then he shifted to the story of Diane Edwards, who was murdered on September 26, 1980. We were told we would hear a taped confession of how the defendant first met Diane, how he abducted her, tied her up, drove to Sherburne County, forced her to have oral sex. When she said something that angered him, he stabbed her twice. He had sex with her dead body, then left.

Jeff Degree presented the opening statement for the defense. There was a murder, he said but this was a case of "who done it?" Who killed Marlys? The convict to whom Ture confessed was a professional snitch tied to a reporter looking for a story. Degree showed the jury the three-page confession, saying that there was no question that Ture signed it, but it was part of a seven-page document that had been analyzed, and the forensic evidence would show there were two inks, that the first ink was the one used to sign the document, that the defendant signed blank pages. Forensic evidence doesn't lie, he told the jury, no matter how often a witness changes his story.

He concluded by saying that Ture was on trial only because of the convict, Toby Krominga, who wrote out the confession. As Degree sat down, I said to Lynn, "He's right. The only reason he is here is because of the confession. The thing is," I added, "it's a true confession."

The state called Fran as its first witness. Though her name was Fran Wohlenhaus-Munday, prosecutor John Fristik called her Ms. Wohlenhaus, to emphasize her relationship to Marlys. Fran calmly answered Fristik's questions about her background, her residence, her marriage to me. She testified for an hour in the morning and over two hours in the afternoon. Ture had been staring at her as she testified, in a way that made it difficult for her to look at him, until she returned his glare, just for a moment. At that point the prosecutor asked if she wanted a break and she said, "I'm fine and ready to keep on." The jury took notice of it all.

On cross-examination, Degree called her Mrs. Munday, talked about her work at the body shop and keeping the books, bringing up her 1982 statement about not knowing the defendant.

On re-direct, Fran talked about her CB radio being on the ledge just inside the door of the house since her car was being repaired at the body shop. Ture's confession described a CB radio in plain sight.

As the parade of witnesses followed Fran, we watched the pieces of a complicated mosaic being put together. Even though we had said for a long time that we would be our own jury and draw our own conclusions, we wanted the evidence to prove Ture's guilt beyond that reasonable doubt. We wanted the jury to act on the proofs of this most important affair. I told Fran, "What really happened in 1979 is no longer the issue; it's what the jury is given and how they come together to reach a verdict."

Angela Oswald, who had been nine at the time of the crime, testified that she saw a car leaving Fran's driveway just a few moments before Fran came home and found Marlys. Her gesture of how she held her bicycle when she saw the car, brought out on cross-examination, seemed like a reenactment of truth. She described the car as a light-colored sporty-type car that sped up when the driver saw her. Ture's written confession said he was driving a white Mustang and spun gravel at a kid on a bike. Another witness testified that he hitchhiked to a bar and was picked up by Ture driving a cream-colored Mustang. Two waitresses picked Ture out of photo lineups, as did one of Marlys's friends. Ray testified that Marlys urgently wanted to tell him something but never got the chance.

Other witnesses placed Ture in Afton, where Marlys was murdered, disclosing other confessions. We heard from a number of witnesses who identified photos at the crime scene, inside and out, and from some of the early investigators. Over and over we were hearing witnesses who would not have been called if we hadn't pushed the investigators and prosecutors to find them and look into their stories.

The pathologist who performed the initial autopsy and the forensic pathologist who made a second autopsy from photographs both concluded that Marlys was murdered by blunt trauma, from a clawlike heavy tool, most likely from seven separate blows. Both also testified using photographs of Marlys after she had been an organ donor. May I say we were saddened by the enlarged, graphic, even lurid photographs of Marlys's body? The justice system needed to expose her, take away her dignity. To restore her honor we had to have justice.

18

A Courthouse, Not a Hall of Justice

WE WERE REWALKING THE PATH OF 1979, and in spite of all our experience with other bereaved parents, even though we thought we knew what to expect, we almost couldn't listen to the horrible words or weigh the ugly evidence. We retreated to the safety of the motor home. We wrote e-mail updates to friends, apologizing for the morbid messages as we sent them.

We barely had strength to go to dinner. Finally we found a comfortable restaurant, ordered good food, drank a glass of wine. When we returned to the motor home, a reply to one e-mail message said, "Please do not apologize for 'morbid' news. By sending your pain to us, perhaps we can then share some of the burden and that of course is what we are called to do. I'm reminded of 'The Servant Song' that we sing at church . . . . 'I will weep when you are weeping. When you laugh, I'll laugh with you. I will share your joy and sorrow till we see this journey through.' Know that your faith community is very much with you."

At a nearby church that next Sunday, the message told us of Christians being called to be faithful. It was this faithfulness from our friends and family that allowed us to recover from the days when we hung on each word of every witness.

During the trial I got to know the reporters covering the case for the two major Twin Cities newspapers. Wayne Wangstad of the St. Paul *Pioneer Press* told me he had covered the Edwards trial. Wangstad wrote a story after Ture was sentenced to a mandatory life term for first-degree murder of Diane Edwards. In an interview with Ture, Wangstad asked him if he knew why he was convicted if he claimed to be innocent, and Ture replied, "My own big mouth got me into this. . . . Even my brother said they would have never charged me if I hadn't confessed."

"Joe," Wangstad asked, "can you imagine yourself as a juror looking at evidence in the Edwards case?"

"If I was like them people on the jury, Goodie Two-Shoes who have never been arrested or had any trouble with the cops, well, I guess if I was like that I guess I would too convict."

"What do you think about the sentence?" Wangstad asked.

"What else can you think?" Ture replied. "It's the regular sentence for murder, just the normal one you get in a cruel case like that. Whoever did it will have to pay for it."

Fran saved this paper because this article quoted Ture as denying the confessions he made to Toby Krominga. "There was nothing on the pages at all, he wanted me to sign my name and date it. Evidently what he did is fill in some other stuff. Now if I was going to confess to any killings, wouldn't I do it with the correct people? I certainly wouldn't do it with any dumb cons," Ture said.

Wangstad wrote, "A question about whether he knew and killed Wohlenhaus brought a smirk to his face and another negative nod of his head."

We knew about that smirk. We had seen tapes of him being interviewed and we had seen him smirk. We had become confident that Ture looked at Marlys with that smirk when he tried to pick her up at Gene Daniels the weekend before he murdered her.

In the next week of the trial, an expert on written documents testified regarding Ture's three-page confession on murdering Marlys and a four-page document in which Ture confessed to killing Alice Huling and three of her children and about which the jury wouldn't be told. After the expert's testimony and the cross-examination, scientific facts were established, but those facts fit a number of interpretations, including Ture signing blank pages or after they contained the confession.

Then Toby Krominga testified for six hours. We knew he was a con man, a multiply convicted felon, but could find no reason why Ture signed the confessions other than because Ture was the murderer. How could Krominga, who had been in jail when Marlys was murdered, get access to the facts in the confessions other than from the one who committed the murders? Maureen Dickenson, Krominga's wife at the time, also testified, as did the television reporter, Tom Matthews, who broke the story, and they convinced us that Krominga could not have made up the facts. Who else would know what Marlys wore that day, or where the Saint Bernard had been locked up, or that the CB sat on the ledge by the side door that the family used? None of that had been made public. The cross-examination of these three key witnesses was extensive, but we believed their sincerity. No motive to lie had been shown.

Ray Lumsden, another former convict—now living a decent life—testified that Ture described the murder weapon in detail, exactly like the tool missing from Fran's house. He described a tool that looked precisely like the forensic pathologist had said it would have to be. Lumsden came forward after he saw Fran on television.

Finally, the prosecution completed its case. We had heard seventy-four witnesses, plus page after page of prior testimony read into the record, tapes and videos of testimony played for the jury; 249 exhibits had been admitted. We heard the shocking story of how Diane Edwards, a bright, pretty, decent young woman, was killed by Ture, via testimony and exhibits from the 1981 jury trial in which Ture was convicted of first-degree murder. Beyond a reasonable doubt. We heard convicts tell us how Ture confessed to this and other murders, and why they came forward: because his attacks on defenseless young women crossed the line of decency, even for the most hardened criminals.

Ture didn't take the stand to testify in Marlys's trial. Early on, Judge Schurrer had warned the jury that there can be no assumption of guilt or innocence if a defendant uses the constitutionally given right not to testify. In his trial for the murder of Diane Edwards, Ture did testify, and most reports we heard were that it was not to his benefit. Here, his defense counsel had been more cautious.

Support for us during the trial had been overwhelmly comforting; it came from old friends, family, new friends, a bailiff whose brother had been murdered, members of the local Parents of Murdered Children chapter. We had e-mail messages from many parts of the United States, and felt love and prayers sustaining us. We had the opportunity to support the Edwards family, to guide the law enforcement officers and lawyers in their work for justice. Prosecutor John Fristik asked Fran if she wanted to give the closing argument—in jest, of course, but also in recognition of how well we knew the case. As we waited for the last days to bring us to a closure of the legal process, subject to any appeals, we looked deep in our own souls for a response.

We were not asked to respond at that time. Judgment was in the hands of the jury as to guilt, and the judge would provide the sentence if guilt was found. Between those two events we would have an opportunity to present a victim impact statement to the court, perhaps to influence the judge as he decided the sentence. It would also give us an opportunity to speak directly to the defendant, though nothing we or anyone else could say or do would bring Marlys and the other victims back to life.

One of our expectations for the trial, in addition to our hope of finally seeing justice done, involved our efforts to have closure with the many suspects we now could believe were innocent. When Tom Cartony testified, not only clearing himself but implicating Ture, and when Special Agent Doolittle corroborated his story, we felt genuine relief. We thanked Tom for coming forward to testify, expressed our sorrow at all he'd endured as a suspect. He thanked us and said it felt good to clear his name. He hoped we would have the answers we sought. Fran hugged him.

In contrast, Fran and I reacted quite badly at first to seeing Greg Loux, her ex-husband, and his two sons, Kevin and Scott, who were called by the defense, along with a handful of other witnesses. As Kevin testified, tension grabbed me in a way that was very different from what I felt when other witnesses testified. When Scott—he and Kevin both used to call Fran "mom"—finished testifying, there came an important release of that tension. Then, in contrast to the time so many years ago at the funeral, Greg testified, and his private, separate agenda no longer made any difference. His testimony and his role in Fran's life no longer had the slightest relevance. A ghost of a most difficult part of our past had been exorcised. Greg, along with a number of others we once suspected, out of fear or anger or in response to what law enforcement told us, really was innocent. What Special Agent Doolittle had told us when he started to really work on the case actually happened: we cleared them, one by one by one, and only the person who killed Marlys remained.

By the end of the morning I wanted to jump up and click my heels with relief. Fran cautioned against celebrating before the verdict, and I agreed, but I had to express the relief I felt. The case was essentially over and would be going to the jury. We knew who was guilty, and we had to believe the evidence would convince the jury.

Friday night we went to the local Parents of Murdered Children chapter meeting in St. Paul. Fran and I, not newly grieving but facing the justice system and its unknowns, sought out others who had been there. As the evening progressed, we offered more comfort than counsel, beginning to see how a court verdict, or the lack of one, was not a magic answer to the pain of loss. For some at the meeting, grief seemed to be confused with the experiences murder-victim families have with the justice system. We offered our theory that the newly bereaved at Compassionate Friends meetings often want to talk with others whose child has died from a similar cause. As time goes by they realize the death of a loved one is by far the overwhelming factor. The details and circumstances are baggage, different for each kind of death but not the dominating factor. Murder shouldn't be different, should it?

Over the weekend, we tried to relax. Closing arguments would be on Tuesday, followed by instructions to the jury, and then we would wait for the verdict. Fran and I decided to have a thank-you party on the day following the charge to the jury, on Wednesday evening. No matter what the jury decided, no matter what sentence the judge might decree, we wanted to thank our friends and those devoted to the case for the work and the accompaniment we had received.

After we found a place, we put together an invitation, took it to a printer, and took off, going for a drive north, along the St. Croix River. It was an almost perfect day, warm enough to have the convertible top down yet cool in the shade, the fall colors in near-full glory. Others too were out on this last day of the season, driving their classic and collectible cars.

We stopped along the river. A man said he envied our convertible and paid for his comment by hearing Fran tell him why we were here, not home in Pennsylvania.

"Did you used to live here?" he asked.

"Yes," she replied.

"I hope your tragedy wasn't the reason you left."

"It was," Fran said, "but we like our new home."

Later, as we drove along a gravel road through a wooded area, Fran said, "I could never, never live in the country again. I love it, but I don't think I could put away my fear." Pointing to homes with little charm and no character, she added, "I love the house we have. I miss the country but I have my garden. I miss Marlys, but I have my memories."

Our waiting had become different, too, no longer impatient. We felt as if time had stopped and wouldn't begin again until we heard the closing arguments as a final review of what we knew.

We had pushed the system, forcing it to respond to our cry for justice, to bring Ture to trial. We tested credibility, looked at bias and motive, analyzed facts and scientific conclusions, heard tapes, watched the defendant. We concluded that he was a serial rapist, a killer of young women. We found ourselves telling each other that he was guilty. We would even ask each other—and ourselves privately—if we had reasonable doubt as to his guilt. Neither of us had any doubt, reasonable or not, that Joe Ture killed Marlys. Now the jury would hear the final words from the lawyers, first from the prosecution and then from the defense.

Representing the state of Minnesota, John Fristik gave the closing argument, holding the jury and everyone else in the courtroom spellbound. After more than two hours of quiet, patient dialogue with the jury, not just speaking to them but engaging them point by point, Fristik finally ended. "Since we started this trial four weeks ago the days have gotten shorter, the air kind of got colder, but the light of justice shines brighter and brighter for Marlys Wohlenhaus. And that light of justice will guide you in your deliberations, I trust."

After a break for lunch, Jeff Degree gave the closing argument for the defense. He brought up all the scientific testimony and exhibits about different inks, different pens, different orders of signing. He placed a lot of weight on the scientific testimony, saying, "Now, ladies and gentlemen, this evidence proves to you what happened. It proves it. There's not a doubt. It's not something you need to think about or worry about." Then, after he finished addressing every point in the written confession of killing Marlys, Degree said, "That's the stupidest story I ever heard. It makes no sense. Unlike the Diane Edwards case, which was horrible and awful and terrible. It made sense. This makes absolutely no sense. It's ridiculous."

Degree concluded his argument by calmly summarizing Marlys's murder as a simple case in which a burglar had entered the house, was surprised by Marlys entering, "and the burglar hit her over the head with the pry bar." He then sat down, not saying why this burglar continued to hit her after she had fallen to the floor.

Fran and I listened intently to both closing arguments and concluded that we knew Joe Ture killed Marlys. So simple, yet we understood how the jury could buy into the defense's efforts to create reasonable doubt. Judge Schurrer gave final instructions to the jury. It would be a while before we would learn if they had heard enough evidence to make this most important decision.

19

What Is Our Reply to Evil?

W HEN THE JURY began their deliberations on Tuesday afternoon, we wandered home, then went to dinner with some of the investigators, now friends. Even though they too were anxious, they helped us to relax, change the subject, talk about their lives for a while. During dinner our ears strained to hear the telephone ring, to have someone say we needed to be at court for a verdict.

Wednesday brought more waiting, and then the thank-you party, a quiet gathering of so many we wanted, even needed, to have with us. Lynn and Ray brought Fran a statue of an angel, and we gave it a temporary place of prominence in the restaurant. At about 8:20 p.m., Captain Mike Johnson came up to Fran and quietly whispered, "We have a verdict." He had just received a call from the court. "Can I tell them?" Fran asked. "This is for real?" I asked. Johnson said yes to both questions.

"We have a verdict and fifteen minutes to get to the courthouse," Fran shouted to the crowd.

Fran and I were among the first to get there, sitting in our regular place in the courtroom, watching and waiting for the jury. Behind us more than fifty family members and friends crowded in anticipation. The defendant, the lawyers, and the judge finally took their places, and the jury walked in, not looking at us, giving no sign of what they had found. While we waited for the clerk to read the verdict, I whispered to Lynn, "Dreams sometimes come true. Sometimes things happen the way they ought to happen." Then we both said, "This is one of those times!"

The clerk slowly read the verdict. "We, the jury, find the defendant guilty of murder in the first degree."

"Thank God!" Fran exclaimed, then she and I resumed our neutral expressions, not showing any emotion, making no sound or gesture of triumph—until we left the courtroom. As soon as we got through the doors, we matched our actions to our feelings about the verdict. I hugged Fran tightly, then we hugged every person we encountered. I felt like I was flying when I went to the press conference Sheriff Frank had announced. Fran beamed her most radiant smile, had one arm around Ray and the other around Lynn as she walked down the hall.

During the press conference, the county attorney and the sheriff answered questions from the media. I felt so proud of Fran in her moment of victory. "Never give up," she said. "Be a squeaky wheel. Encourage law enforcement to bring justice to other families." This victory—in Washington County, Minnesota, for one victim and so many of her family—brought smiles to so many faces, joy to everyone's heart.

At the end of the press conference, when the television teams had left, I added a thought, speaking to the friends and family members who remained with us to the end. I told them about the stone statue of an angel, given to Fran at the party, and how it included a beautiful card signed by Ray, Marlys, and Lynn. "Now," I said, "we feel the presence of our angel in heaven, beaming her beautiful smile down on us." We never asked Lynn or Ray who signed Marlys's name.

On the day of sentencing, we gathered in the courtroom for the last time. Ture and one of his lawyers sat, awaiting judgment. Some of the investigators sat in the jury box to get a better view of the man they had tracked down and put away, they hoped for life. The judge had given permission for us to make victim impact statements, and we decided I'd go first, then Ray and Lynn together, then Fran, who wanted the last word.

When I walked up to the witness box, the judge asked me to introduce myself "for the record." Then I spoke, introducing our whole family, thanking those I could remember to name for all they had done to bring about that moment. I looked Ture directly in the eyes, and he turned away. Near the end of my statement, I spoke about being at a friend's home at dinner in the St. Croix Valley just a few days earlier. Our host asked what I thought about the existence of evil. I quoted my answer for the judge: "Evil people—the defendant in particular—are like an out-of-control fire killing innocent people who, for some reason, even bad luck, don't get out of its way. Some people are truly dangerous, unable to feel any compassion for another, no more than burning trees do for a person trapped and burned to death.

"A forest fire has to be contained, as does this defendant. In his own words, as we heard on tape during the trial, he has admitted, 'It probably is easier to kill again once you done it.'" Then I walked between the two tables separating prosecution and defense, looked again at Ture, who still avoided my eyes, and took my place with Fran.

Lynn stood with Ray as he read her statement, prefacing his reading by saying that the court wouldn't want him to say what he thought. Ray also looked the now convicted defendant in the eyes, and again Ture avoided the stare.

Finally, after so many years of facing the unknown, Fran walked up to the witness box, where once she had told her story, now able to put the final touches on a long, long quest for justice. She gave a loving testimony of Marlys's goodness, contrasted with the evil the defendant had done to her and so many others. Fran closed her statement by saying, "Your Honor, I ask in the name of my daughter Marlys Ann Wohlenhaus that Joseph Ture Jr. be given maximum punishment—to the fullest extent permitted by law—to protect innocent young women so their lives will not be destroyed by his evil acts."

After Fran sat down, Judge Schurrer gave Ture a chance to speak. Ture denied this murder and that of Diane Edwards. Schurrer sentenced Ture to life in prison, to begin after the life sentence for killing Diane Edwards.

There is a surprise ending to our struggle to find Marlys's murderer and have him punished. For some reason, perhaps because we asked for prayer or by the power of prayer for us, we have overcome our hatred for the killer; we are glad for justice and mercy. At first, after the verdict and our opportunity to give victim impact statements, we weren't sure how to react. We were disoriented. Weeks of absent-minded mistakes, confusion, and general lethargy followed. But at our church, among our many friends, we were able to relax. We continued to be a squeaky wheel, and with articles in newspapers and visits to St. Cloud, Minnesota, we embarrassed a county attorney into charging Joe Ture with the Huling murders.

And we are no longer afraid. If you ask Fran how her fear went away, she will tell you it is because Minnesota, or Marlys, seemed to be saying that living in the country would be safe. She will count the events on her fingers. "One. Joe Ture was indicted for the first-degree murders of Alice Huling and her children Susie, Patti, and Wayne. That happened on May 10, 1999, exactly twenty years to the day after Marlys died. Two. Ture's trial for the Huling murders started on January 11, 2000, Marlys's thirty-ninth birthday. Three. The judge sentenced Ture to four additional consecutive life sentences, with those terms to begin on the day he had been indicted, again May 10, 1999. He received his sentence for the Huling murders on February 7, 2000, on his own forty-seventh birthday." The only thing Fran ever said to Joe Ture was at that sentencing hearing in St. Cloud, when she wished him happy birthday.

In 2001 we moved twelve hundred miles from suburban blue-collar Philadelphia to rural Isanti County, Minnesota. We left a sixty-foot-wide lot for fourteen acres and 787 feet of shore on Long Lake, one of two Long Lakes in the county and 157 in the state. We built a house in the woods, past a creek only we can cross. We have transplanted white pines and spruce, planted bulbs and flowers we brought from Pennsylvania, moved old dock sections for a bog walk to be built some day. Running cedar and yard-tall ferns abound, and three bald eagles fish the lake. We have gone from garden and order to nature and randomness.

The opposite has happened in our lives. We have simplified, eliminated extra stuff, no longer subject to the uncertainty of the justice system that claimed our time and energy. We celebrate our victory over death. We won by not letting a murderer take any more victims, not letting him destroy our lives. We have found peace. As Fran says, "We did the last thing on earth we could for Marlys."

Acknowledgments

I COULD NOT HAVE WRITTEN THIS BOOK without the help of many people, and I want to thank them. There would not even have been a complete story to tell without the three-legged stool of dedicated investigators, sympathetic reporters, and our family's determination to have justice for Marlys.

Law enforcement personnel who worked on the case include Washington County Sheriff Jim Frank, Captain Mike Johnson, Deputies Jeff Klarich, Dale Fuerstenberg, and Jim Richter, and BCA Senior Special Agent Everett Doolittle and Special Agent Randy Striker. Together they solved Marlys's case because they persevered rather than let the file sit on a shelf to gather dust. Before the indictment, Washington County Attorney Dick Arney put his office to work. Attorneys Rick Hodsdon and John Fristik did a masterful job in prosecuting to conviction.

Stan Hubbard of KSTP gave publicity and offered reward money early in the investigation. John Gillstrom of the *Stillwater Gazette* kept Marlys before the people in the St. Croix Valley for fifteen years. Tom Hauser of KSTP brought Marlys to the greater metropolitan Twin Cities audience. CBS producer Loen Kelly and reporter Erin Moriarity made the crime a national event on *48 Hours* and found other critical witnesses. Jim Adams of the Minneapolis-based *Star Tribune,* Wayne Wangstad of the St. Paul *Pioneer Press,* and Dave Unze of the

Saint Cloud Times fairly reported on the trials and listened to us when we discussed their writing.

Each of these two essential groups did their best, but they both admit that the third crucial force in solving Marlys's murder was her mother. Fran Wohlenhaus-Munday and the rest of our family and friends who lived with the unsolved murder refused to accept the lack of action and pressed on without giving up. Marlys's brother, Ray Wohlenhaus, and her sister, Lynn Winger, stayed the course to the end, joining in a victim impact statement at the trial. Marlys's high school friends Becky Kirkpatrick, Denise Eisinger, and Beth Campbell remained in touch with Fran and with the investigators, helping their friend and preserving her memories. My children, JD Munday, Maria Stine, and Shawn Munday, understand what we have done. They, too, are victims who struggled with these past twenty years.

After the verdict, and the Huling verdicts, and after Ture dropped his appeal in Marlys's case and lost his appeal from the Huling convictions, we thought we were done with the justice system. Then, in 2003, a public defender brought a Motion for a New Trial in Marlys's case. The district court denied the motion, and Ture appealed to the Minnesota Supreme Court. On June 3, 2004, that court affirmed the lower court. We followed the appeals closely, of course, and were amazed at how much anxiety we felt. And relief that now all possible legal doors have been closed.

I am extremely grateful for the opportunity to tell how we refused to allow violent crime to go unpunished. Not only Marlys's family but also those who loved and mourned Diane Edwards, Alice Huling, Susie Huling, Patti Huling, Wayne Huling, and Joan Bierschbach have been able to be heard and to proclaim their own need for justice.

I am pleased to acknowledge the instruction, advice, and encouragement I received from the writers who have seen some or all of this work. Bill Wartman got me started when I still lived in Pennsylvania. Patricia Hoolihan, Cheri Register, and Nolan Zavoral helped shape the manuscript and provided much advice as the drafts piled up. My "six other writers" group at the Loft Literary Center in Minneapolis has included Art, Cheryll, Cynthia, John, Linda, Maureen, Rusty, and Sue. They gave me encouragement and fair criticism. Folks at the University of Minnesota Press took the story to completion, with kind suggestions from Todd Orjala, Laura Westlund, and Lynn Marasco.

Most of all I want to thank my wife, Fran Wohlenhaus-Munday, who taught me to see the positive in all of life. Together, we remember Marlys.

JOHN S. MUNDAY, a lawyer, has also studied theology, and he received a graduate degree from Princeton Theological Seminary. He is the author of *Surviving the Death of a Child* and a contributing editor to *Grief Digest*. He and his wife, Fran Wohlenhaus-Munday, are active supporters of bereaved parents; they present workshops at national conferences of The Compassionate Friends, Inc., the In Loving Memory Foundation, and Parents of Murdered Children. They now live in Isanti, Minnesota, where John writes a weekly column, "Let's Talk about Grief," for the *Isanti County News*.